D0638663

The Depression in
Canadian literature

THEMES IN CANADIAN LITERATURE
General Editor *David Arnason*

The Depression in Canadian Literature

Edited by
Alice K. Hale and Sheila A. Brooks

Macmillan of Canada

Themes in Canadian Literature

The Artist in Canadian Literature edited by Lionel Wilson
Canadian Humour and Satire edited by Theresa Ford
Canadian Myths and Legends edited by Michael O. Nowlan
The Depression in Canadian Literature edited by Alice K. Hale
    and Sheila Brooks
The French Canadian Experience edited by Gaston Saint-Pierre
The Frontier Experience edited by Jack Hodgins
The Immigrant Experience edited by Leuba Bailey
Isolation in Canadian Literature edited by David Arnason
The Maritime Experience edited by Michael O. Nowlan
Native Peoples in Canadian Literature edited by William and
    Christine Mowat
The Ontario Experience edited by John Stevens
The Prairie Experience edited by Terry Angus
The Role of Woman in Canadian Literature edited by Elizabeth
    McCullough
The Search for Identity edited by James Foley
The Urban Experience edited by John Stevens
The West Coast Experience edited by Jack Hodgins

© 1976 The Macmillan Company of Canada Limited
70 Bond Street, Toronto M5B 1X3
Affiliated with Maclean-Hunter Learning Materials Company.

ISBN 0-7705-1365-4

Canadian Cataloguing in Publication Data

Main entry under title:
The Depression in Canadian literature
(Themes in Canadian literature)
Bibliography: p.
ISBN 0-7705-1365-4 pa.
1. Depressions — 1929 — Canada.   2. Canadian literature (English) — 20th century.*   I. Hale, Alice K., date   II. Brooks, Sheila, date   III. Series.
PS8249.D47   C810'.8'0052   C76-017063-0
PR9194.9.D47

Printed in Canada

ACKNOWLEDGMENTS

Grateful acknowledgment is made for the use of copyright material.

Photographs: p. 8, Public Archives of Canada; p. 13, Archives of Saskatchewan; p. 34, Archives of Saskatchewan; p. 35, Toronto Star Syndicate; p. 59, Canadian Forces Photograph; p. 63, Archives of Saskatchewan; p. 77, U.S.D.A. Photograph; p. 79, Toronto Star Syndicate; p. 87, Public Archives of Canada; p. 90, Archives of Saskatchewan; p. 101, Canadian National Railways; p. 110, International Harvester Company of Canada Ltd.

Aquarius: "To a Generation Unemployed" from *Canadian Poetry*, Vol. 1, No. 4, March 1937.

Arthur S. Bourinot: "Outcasts" from *The Collected Poems of Arthur S. Bourinot* (1947). Reprinted by permission.

Barry Broadfoot: Excerpts from *Ten Lost Years*, copyright © 1973 by Barry Broadfoot. Reprinted by permission of Doubleday & Company, Inc.

Morley Callaghan: "The Blue Kimono" from *Morley Callaghan's Stories*, The Macmillan Company of Canada Limited.

James H. Gray: "The Golden Age of Boondoggling" from *The Winter Years* by James H. Gray, The Macmillan Company of Canada Limited.

Linda Grayson and Michael Bliss (eds.): Mrs. Franklin's letters as quoted in *The Wretched of Canada*, University of Toronto Press, 1971. Mr. Bennett's letter reprinted by permission of the Harriet Irving Library, University of New Brunswick.

Mary Quayle Innis: "Holiday" from *Canadian Forum*, January 1932. Reprinted by permission.

A. M. Klein: "Friends, Romans, Hungrymen" from *New Frontier* magazine, Vol. 1, No. 1, April 1936. Reprinted by permission of the Author's estate.

Margaret Laurence: "Horses of the Night" from *A Bird in the House* by Margaret Laurence. Reprinted by permission of The Canadian Publishers, McClelland and Stewart Limited, Toronto.

Kenneth Leslie: "Two Thieves" from *The Poems of Kenneth Leslie*, The Ladysmith Press, 1971. Reprinted by permission.

Dorothy Livesay: "Day and Night" from *Collected Poems: The Two Seasons* by Dorothy Livesay. Reprinted by permission of McGraw-Hill Ryerson Limited.

Anne Marriott: "Prairie" from *Canadian Forum*, May 1938. Reprinted by permission of the Author.

Alice Munro: "Walker Brothers Cowboy" from *Dance of the Happy Shades* by Alice Munro. Reprinted by permission of McGraw-Hill Ryerson.

Alden Nowlan: "It's Good To Be Here" from *Saturday Night*, July /August 1975. Reprinted by permission of the Author.

Henry Paul: "I Am a Transient" from *Canadian Forum*, May 1939.

F. R. Scott: "Credit" from *Canadian Forum*, March 1935; and "Efficiency: 1935". Reprinted by permission of the Author.

A. J. M. Smith: "News of the Phoenix" from *A. J. M. Smith: Poems New and Collected*. Reprinted by permission of Oxford University Press, Canada.

Raymond Souster: "Hunger" (1944). Reprinted by permission of the Author.

CONTENTS

INTRODUCTION

It left its mark on many a good man today, let me tell you. . . . The wounds of war leave scars, but the wounds of humiliation and lost pride leave their scars here, up here in the mind. . . .

from *Ten Lost Years*, ed., Barry Broadfoot

The Great Depression dates from the stock-market crash of October 24, 1929, although ominous signs had appeared earlier — overproduction of wheat and industrial goods, drought on the Prairies that summer, and exuberant buying from door-to-door stock salesmen. Recovery began in some areas in 1937 and 1938, but only the Second World War finally ended the Depression. During these ten years, Canada suffered as much as any country in the world.

In the worst year, 1933, official Canadian unemployment figures ranged from 20 per cent to 50 per cent in some urban areas. In human terms, one in five families was without support and as many as two million of Canada's ten million people were without income.

These were indeed the Hungry Thirties. Although prices were low — bread 5c a loaf, a suit $12, a modest house $4,000 — those who were employed often had their wages cut. Women in garment factories received as little as 16c an hour; few people earned as much as $25 a week, considered a satisfactory wage.

Unemployment insurance and family allowances did not exist. Relief, one of the most degrading features of the Depression, was difficult to get. For the pittance received, families often had to give up their driving licence, telephone, and liquor permit to ensure that they spent money only on absolute necessities. Frequently, vouchers for food and fuel were given rather than cash. Those who were required to work for their relief payments too often found that their work had no function — "boondoggling", as James Gray describes it, meant building roads that went nowhere, digging dandelions, or moving rocks from one pile to another. Under such demoralizing conditions life became a grinding struggle merely to survive.

Many people received no welfare. Men and boys roamed the country futilely looking for work. They rode the rails and lived in hobo camps, hounded out of towns. Relief camps, intended to keep potential trouble-makers away from the cities, were set up in

1

isolated areas where single men worked for 20c a day, under strict military supervision.

Canada's southern Prairies suffered more than any other area of the world. For the farmers there, the Dirty Thirties meant seemingly endless years of drought, grasshopper plagues, and near famine. Each spring hope returned; each year was worse as no rain fell. Anne Marriott's classic poem, "The Wind Our Enemy", found in many anthologies, captures exactly the frustration and despair of those who stayed and those who abandoned their farms.

In seeking to explain their plight, some people blamed immigrants for taking jobs needed by Canadians; the government, in response to public demand, deported thousands. In Montreal, the Jews were openly accused by Mayor Houde of being responsible for Canada's problems. Other people saw wealthy Prime Minister R. B. Bennett as the arch-villain. Cars drawn by horses because the owners could not afford gas were contemptuously called "Bennett buggies". Too late, Bennett introduced unemployment insurance and minimum-wage legislation. He was defeated by Mackenzie King's Liberals in the election of 1935.

The desperate conditions of the Thirties were bound to have important political effects. Many Canadians saw the Depression as proof that the capitalist system had failed. The CCF party, forerunner of the NDP, was founded on the basis of social concern. The Social Credit party emerged on the Prairies. For some, the Communist party offered hope. The search for solutions permanently changed the political nature of Canada.

The literature produced during the Depression was most often concerned with social and political criticism. In this anthology Frank Scott and A. M. Klein satirize, and Dorothy Livesay harshly attacks, an uncaring, degrading industrial system. Morley Callaghan is only one of the novelists who, in fictionalizing the victims of the Depression, produced works of lasting literary and historical value. And "the wretched of Canada" themselves are represented here through their letters and personal accounts.

Three decades after it ended, Canadians found renewed interest in the Depression era. Time permits greater objectivity and assessment, and today's writers, such as Margaret Laurence and Alice Munro, reveal to all of us the hardship and magnificent courage of those years — years that have indeed left scars but have also enriched our literature and our very identity.

Alice K. Hale and Sheila A. Brooks

2

HOLIDAY
Mary Quayle Innis

Riding in the car had made her a little faint and unsteady, but now that she was safely inside the big store Mrs. Samchuk felt better. My, it was a long time since she had been here — two months anyhow — and such a lot as she had been through. She had earned a holiday. Lydie and Dolly and Jim would be all right with Mrs. Jenkins to keep an eye on them till Pete got home. It was silly, Pete tramping from house to house looking for work when there wasn't any. Miles he walked to cut a lawn or carry out ashes for fifteen cents. It just used up his shoes and brought back that pain in his leg where he got hurt in the war. He'd do better to look after the kids and let her get out oftener. But now she was out and she meant to stay a while. She lifted the baby higher in her arms and shuffled along the aisle to the cosmetic counter.

It was one of her favourites. The smells were lovely and the colours made it like a garden. The powder boxes were gold and red and green and black, and there were bottles of bath salts, sparkling pink and lavender, and cakes of soap in the shape of roses and swans. Everything glittered like fire. Even the powder puffs were peach and pink and the little rouge boxes were like rubies. Nettie Samchuk walked round the counter very slowly. She didn't dare touch anything but nobody could stop her looking and smelling the thick, bright scents. It was a wonder some of the homely, old-looking women who bought silver powder boxes and huge pink puffs. You'd think such things would be for young girls but very likely the old ones needed them more.

A salesgirl at the corner of the counter sprayed a lady with perfume out of a tall crystal atomizer and a few of the tiny drops fell sparkling on Nettie's shoulder. She smiled and sniffed them appreciatively. That was nice. Rose, it smelled like, though you couldn't tell. They had such funny names.

Over here were the crepe paper flowers and in the corner the paints and coloured paper for artists. She had liked to paint in school; if she had a paint box now she could dabble in it when the kids were in bed. Suppose the Charities woman found her with a paint box. Nettie almost laughed. Anyhow she was too tired at night to do anything but sleep. For a while she looked at silk stockings and handkerchiefs, gay as flowers, and purses with fancy clasps and your initial cut out of gold and fastened on the corner. Then she took the elevator upstairs. A woman in a big brown fur stared at her and frowned but when she saw the baby she made room. Nettie looked right back at her, not rude but not scared either. A store was for everybody.

Children's clothes — that was another of the places she liked. Of course if she had any money she would go to the basement where the things were that you could really buy, but having none she liked better to stick to places that didn't tempt her. Her favourite game was to dress her children. From the show cases you could choose outfits for all of them and the possibility of having such fine things was too remote to allow any sensation of envy. Mrs. Samchuk leaned against the edge of the counter, letting the baby's body rest on it while she selected Lydie's costume. That flowered dress with smocking across the front would be swell on Lydie with one of those pale pink angora tams that looked so soft you wanted to put your face against it. And white shoes and stockings. Lydie hadn't ever had white. She'd be lucky now if she had any colour. Dolly would look cute in that red knitted outfit with white ducks on the jersey. She moved slowly round the counter staring with fascinated eyes. That blue romper marked "Made in France" would be real sweet on Jim. The women in France must have good eyes to do that tiny cross stitch. It made Nettie blink to look at it.

There were stools before the counter and, seeing no clerk near, she sat down gingerly and swung her aching feet free of the floor. These shoes hurt her terribly. They were the right size, too. The lady she worked for last fall had given them to her and she had been delighted because they were her own number. Funny how shoes could hurt when they were the right size. Anyhow they did; the soles of her feet were like a burning fire. She sagged all over resting her tired back and arms, for though the baby was light, still, carrying him made her arms cramped and stiff. Quite a pretty shawl the Charities woman

4

had given her for him and the dress wasn't bad, only a little yellow around the neck. The bonnet was too big, though, and made his dark, tiny face look like a withered apple. Funny how such a mite of a baby could make you such a lot of pain. He slept so quietly you would almost be worried if you hadn't had babies before, thinking there was something wrong with him.

"Would you like to look at anything, madam?"

The salesgirl had come up without Nettie's seeing and her voice was icily sarcastic. Horrid little snip. Nettie got off the stool with dignity and walked away, not hurrying, to show that she was as good as anybody. Well, there was a lot ahead of her, she had better be getting on. It would be more pleasure if she weren't quite so tired and shaky but it was something to remember anyway, a real treat for anybody that was kept in so close.

The dresses and hats she had been looking forward to. But no mother of four children could get into a dress like that green one, not if her corset was as rickety as Nettie's. No hips at all to them and the models looked about seven feet tall. That blue velvet one with a cream lace vest — if that wasn't the grandest thing! Nettie's mouth opened in a kind of gape of rapture. The way the skirt swept out in deep blue folds right to the floor. You'd have to have swell slippers with diamond buckles. What would Pete say if he saw her in a dress like that. She sighed and hitched the baby upward again. He kept slipping down so, as if her arms were not strong enough to hold him.

Pete hadn't seen her look nice since the year they were married. This green and orange print she had on was faded to a bilious yellow and her red dress at home wasn't much better. Ma had told her she wouldn't have anything if she married a foreigner like Pete Samchuk. But he had such black eyes and she hadn't paid any attention to Ma. Well, he had done his best. They were on the Charities but still they were a lot better off than some. Mrs. Jenkins' husband had left her and Mrs. Knebel's was dead of pneumonia only last month and her with eight children and expecting again. You couldn't complain when you had your man even if he didn't earn fifty cents some weeks.

Those little hats that sat on one side of your head like a doughnut were kind of cute. For herself Nettie felt she would prefer the good old pull-down kind. The one she had on had been given to her by a lady she worked for when Dolly was a baby. It was all out of shape now, if it had ever had a shape, and was the colour of the ground, but you always knew you had it on and that it wouldn't slide off unexpectedly. May Jenkins had one of these new one-sided hats with her hair all waved where the hat wasn't. It looked cute on her but the wonder was, with Mr. Jenkins gone and May out of work these three months, where the girl found money to pay for it. Likely there was something queer about it. Mrs. Jenkins better keep an eye on her. Nettie took the elevator again.

Here were the hammocks and swings and the sight was too tempting. She slipped in cautiously among them and sat down on a huge sliding couch covered with striped denim. The baby stirred fretfully as she laid him in her lap but he did not cry. My, but it was grand to sit down a minute. Her back was one grinding pain. She lifted one burning foot off the floor and then the other. If you had a couch like this you'd have a swell garden to put it in with grass and flower beds and a shiny silver ball like the one that had been displayed in the store window. Nettie didn't know what they were for but they would look nice with the sun shining on them.

The floor walker was coming. Nettie saw him but she couldn't gather up the baby and get to her feet in time.

"It's against the rules to sit on the couches," he said sharply.

She moved obediently away. It hadn't been much of a rest but she had as good as seen the green garden with the silver ball in the middle of it.

Groceries. That was another good place. It made you hungry, if you hadn't been hungry before, to see the piles of polished apples, the bright oranges, and pale grapefruit. Then the moist pink cuts of meat and the long marble counter ranged with cheeses and the fascinating wire the man used to cut them. And cakes iced with roses and "happy birthday" in pink, and the crusty brown rolls. Nettie sighed and leaned against the glass case with a sudden horrible empty feeling. A girl in white was demonstrating a jelly powder, serving out portions of sparkling orange jelly in white fluted paper cups, but she pretended not to see Mrs. Samchuk who lingered a little and then hunched the baby up and started on.

That potato salad looked nice now with curls of lettuce all round it and a flower on top made of bits of beet and olive. The Charities' food was all right but a body got tired of oatmeal and beans and turnips and no meat but stewing beef. The kids never liked porridge but they had to get used to it now right enough. Nettie couldn't bear the sight of it herself, but you couldn't complain, at least not to the Charities.

Should she go to the rest room and sit down a while? It would be nice but maybe she'd had enough for today. Pete would be home and the kids fussing. She took the elevator down. Her forehead was all over sweat and really if she had been that kind of a person Nettie would have thought she was going to faint. But once she got into the air she'd be all right. While she was hurrying toward a door, a dreadful thing happened. A tall, horse-faced woman in a mannish suit stood in front of her suddenly, demanding, in a loud, terrifying voice,

"How old is that baby?"

Nettie was so startled that she could only stare and mutter, "Two weeks."

"Two weeks! Don't you know you haven't any business to bring a baby as young as that into a place full of germs? Somebody ought to see about it. I never heard of such a thing. I don't see —"

Nettie opened her mouth to tell the woman what she thought of her for interfering with a decent, respectable person, but she felt all at once too tired, too helplessly weak to say a word. Instead she plodded around the tall woman and reached the door.

She was trembling all over. The horrible, prying woman had spoiled all her pleasure. Now she couldn't go home till she saw something nice to take the bad taste out of her mouth. And here it was, in the display window right beside her. Under a white and silver arch stood a bride with a satin train yards long and a veil, cold and cloudy white like a snowstorm. Those looked like real lillies in her hands only of course they couldn't be. Made awfully good, though, to fool a person like that. Nettie's curved arms holding the baby sagged slowly downward while she gazed. Then someone brushed against her and she sighed and hoisted the bundle to the level of her breast.

One hand fumbled for the streetcar ticket in the pocket of her sweater. No need to carry a purse when that was all she had. The car stop was on the other side of the street. She took her place in the crowd at the corner to wait for the green light. Her knees bent under her with weariness, but she thought that when they saw the baby someone would give her a seat in the car. The kids would be crying and she would have to hurry with their supper. Never mind. She could go on now for a while. She had had her holiday.

From THE WRETCHED OF CANADA
Linda Grayson and Michael Bliss (eds.)

Kent, Ont.
December 15, 1931.

Hon. R. B. Bennett
Royal York, Toronto

Dear Mr. Bennett, — I hope you will pardon my writing to you today.

I saw in the *Toronto Star* where you were going to be the speaker on Wednesday night at the Royal York so have taken the liberty to write to you and I hope you will regard this as strictly confidential.

I am glad you arrived home safely from your trip abroad and hope it has done you good.

Would like to hear your talk but have no radio.

You will wonder what in the world I have written to you about.

Well, we are farmers. We came out to this place about five years ago to try our hand at farming.

My man has a trade at carpentering but he developed rheumatism in the shoulders, caused I believe by the constant use of hammer and saw, so we thought a change of work, using other muscles might be good for him.

We traded our home, equity 2300. on this farm but found after moving here that the place had been terribly neglected and was in a very run down condition. We have worked very hard and it shows a marked improvement but we seem unable to get far ahead.

There are several buildings which could be renovated but the folks who hold the mortgages will not let us tear them away to improve the rest and we feel it is not fair for us to put on improvements, not having the privilege of using what could be used here as well.

Last year I sent $12. to the Agricultural Development Board asking for a loan but they replied they were sorry they could not let us have it but *hoped* we could get it somewhere else. Now, Mr. Bennett, I ask you, what is the use of trying to get on if the Government refuses help to their own Canadian-born sons and daughters. I suppose if we were Doukobours, Emigrants or most anything else, we would be set up and given a chance. We have done all we can to be decent, honourable, and to raise our family to be a credit to the country, but what's the use. On every hand we get a knock. What I want to do is get a start with chickens. We had a lovely flock when on No. 7 Highway but after Mother died I had to go home for a while and one Sunday night — while my husband came to see us — some person came and took everything. We have lost heart but I am beginning again to get a flock together. There is a wonderful range here for hens and geese but I think we will be having a foreclosure soon and so hardly know what to do. The boys, our boys are twins 13 years old, want us to stay on the farm, but I am afraid we will have no choice in the matter. Today, if it were to save my life, I could not find one cent in the place. We own a note at the Bank for $150. and one would imagine from the fuss that is made over it, that it was $150,000.

The worry of all these things is driving me mad. God alone knows how hard we have tried to get on but prices are no good now. If we could borrow about $10,000. at 3 per cent and pay off what we owe to everybody we would still have plenty to fix up our farm and get a start in chickens and a few good cows. We have all our implements paid for and have 3 cows, 1 heifer, 3 horses and a colt 1½ yrs old, and all we owe on them is $50. altogether. We have had to sell our two other young cows and two good sows to pay up but thank goodness we are that much farther out of debt.

Ours is I suppose only one case in hundreds but nevertheless it doesn't alter our worries any. Is there nothing that can be done to help out such cases? The unemployment situation is as bad on the farms as anywhere but we never receive help in any way. Christmas is only 10 days away and I haven't the first thing for any of the youngsters and have nothing to get anything with. Many times I have been tempted to throw everything to the winds but something still seems to whisper

"Keep on". What a wonderful thing Faith in God is. There is a little verse which seems to mean so much to me.

Courage, brother, do not stumble
Tho the path be dark as night
There's a star to guide the humble
Trust in God, and do the right.

Tho the road be dark and dreary
And the ending out of sight.
Step out boldly, glad or weary,
Trust in God, and do the right.

Isn't it beautiful? Please God I may always remember and do just that. Trust in God, and do the right.

Please Mr. Bennett, forgive me for sending this letter but somehow it eases my mind to send it.

I hope you have a very Merry Christmas.

Respectfully yours,
Dorothy Franklin

[Reply]

Ottawa, December 29, 1931.

Dear Mrs. Franklin:

I cannot tell you how greatly I was concerned after reading your very excellent letter. It was the letter of a woman who had endured much, but had still maintained her courage and faith.

I have ventured to write the Minister of Agriculture at Toronto to see if something cannot be done to assist your family.

I regret the delay in answering you, but the truth is I dictated a reply the day your letter was received, but the notes were mislaid and it is only this morning that I was advised of that fact.

I trust the New Year may bring you great happiness and be

an entire change to the one you have just passed. With all good wishes and kindest regards, I am,

Yours faithfully,
R. B. Bennett

Brechin, Ont. Feb. 28, 1935.

I hope you will pardon me for writing to you but I feel that, as the head of our country you should be made acquainted with some of the things we of the poorer class are up against. Oh, I know you have all kinds of this stuff thrown at you but today I just have to unload. You may recall that I wrote to you about three years ago and you very kindly interceded for a farm loan for us at Kent, but to no effect. We were refused the loan and the mortgage was foreclosed and we lost everything. We made a sale to pay the taxes and I reserved about thirty P. R. Hens that were laying and the only bit of money we had coming in. Well, the sale day was terribly stormy and along with other things on that day, there was a very poor turnout. The sale amounted to $220. for what we had paid $770. and the $220. was $24. less than the taxes. So my hens were sold at 80c each, which paid up the taxes and left us with nothing. When you wrote to me you said you hoped that year would be our best. Well, perhaps it was. It left us nothing but our experience and that has been dearly bought. We lost $3500. — a mere nothing to some perhaps but our life's work. We moved to the front here hoping things might be better but since Dec. 10th, my man has been able to bring in $3.00. He is out every day looking for work and always the same results. Yesterday he came home and told me there is some road work starting next week but in order to get on, the men must sign up for relief. I wonder why men who are self-respecting have to be subjected to such humiliation and embarrassment when they are only too willing to work if possible. It isn't only the men who suffer but the families of these men. We have a pair of twin boys, sixteen years old. Both at school yet but those boys have gone all winter without underwear and no overcoats and do not even own a suit of

12

clothes. They are wearing the same pants and sweaters week day
and Sunday. I have to mend and wash their pullovers so they are
presentable for Sunday School but they will not go to church
because they are so shabby. We were taught to believe God put
us women here for the noble cause of Motherhood. I wonder
how many would have suffered what we have, had we known
our children were not even going to have the necessities of life.
This week we have bought just 1 lb. of butter & 3 loaves of
bread. I'm ashamed to ask the grocer for any more credit. We
have been eating stew. First potatoes & carrots and then carrots
and potatoes. I'm so discouraged. I wonder which requires the
greater courage, to carry on knowing how much we are all
needing and cannot have or to end it all as that poor woman did
this week in Oakville by sticking her head in a pail of water and
drowning. My last coat that I bought was eight years ago for
the fabulous sum of $10.75c and my Sunday dress is an old one
of a cousin's made over. I wouldn't feel so badly if we only had
our home but having no prospect of ever having anything is
killing me. The people around this gritty hole are saying "Wait
until the new government gets in." It's all bosh. No party alone
can change things much. My idea is that all must work together

to accomplish much good. In trouble such as the country is labouring under now, the partyism should be forgotten for the good of all mankind. Yes, I'm Tory to my toes but just the same I have no hard feelings toward those who think differently from me. Some day things will turn out all right and I am very thankful that through it all I can truthfully say I can still maintain my faith and trust in God above.

Forgive me if I have taken too much of your time. Yours respectfully,

Dorothy Franklin

Brechin, Ont. March 18, 1935.

Hon. R. B. Bennett.

Dear Mr. Bennett, — Will you please accept my grateful thanks for the Twenty Dollars you sent me last week for the twins. I told our Minister that I had received a gift to get needed articles for them and he said he and his wife were going in to Toronto the next day and would take us along with them. I got each boy a suit of clothes and a hat for the money you sent and if you could have seen the expression of mingled pleasure and pride which overcame their faces when they got ready for Sunday School yesterday you would have been glad it was in your power to give such joy to a couple of boys.

I washed and ironed their ties and had their shoes mended and when they came to me with a kiss and "You're a pal Mother", well, it just meant everything to me. It isn't very good grammar but it is their expression of gratitude.

I hope, Mr. Bennett, that your health will soon be restored to you.

Again thanking you and wishing you the very best of luck.

I remain
Yours respectfully
Dorothy Franklin

POMPOUS, SMUG, AND RICH
Barry Broadfoot (ed.)

"Mr. Bennett was pompous, smug, and rich. He had the most prestigious law firm in Calgary, and could pick and choose his clients. No, he was not a man of the people. I could never say that. I don't think he knew a thing about the Canadian people. No, even after four years in office, as prime minister, I don't think he knew anything about the people.

I'll tell you a story which might tell you something about him. He bought a new car, the jazziest in Calgary, and while he was learning to drive it he ran it up a pole. He walked away from it, and as far as I know he never got behind the wheel of a car again.

Nobody could talk to him at any time and he had a secretary named Miss Miller and you needed eight master keys to get by her. He never married. Why? Well, I can't answer that, and I don't know of any kids he's got running around here either.

I do know that the biggest shock of his life was when he was defeated in '35. He couldn't believe it. Everybody else knew it was coming, but he was so arrogant, so far from the true state of affairs concerning the people that he just didn't believe it could happen. It came to him as a terrible shock. That's the kind of man he was."

EFFICIENCY: 1935
F. R. Scott

The efficiency of the capitalist system
Is rightly admired by important people.
Our huge steel mills
Operating at 25% of capacity
Are the last word in organization.
The new grain elevators
Stored with superfluous wheat
Can load a grain-boat in two hours.
Marvellous card-sorting machines
Make it easy to keep track of the unemployed.
There is not one unnecessary worker
In these textile plants
That require a 75% tariff protection.
And when our closed shoe-factories re-open
They will produce more footwear than we can possibly buy.
So don't let us start experimenting with socialism
Which everyone knows means inefficiency and waste.

THE BLUE KIMONO
Morley Callaghan

It was hardly more than dawn when George woke up so
suddenly. He lay wide awake listening to a heavy truck moving
slowly on the street below; he heard one truck-driver shout
angrily to another; he heard a hundred small street sounds
multiplying and rolling with the motion of the city awakening.

For many mornings in the last six months George had lain
awake waiting to hear all the noises of people preparing to go to
work, the noises of doors slamming, of women taking in the
milk, of cars starting, and sometimes, later on in the morning,
he had wondered where all these people went when they hurried
out briskly with so much assurance.

Each morning he awakened a little earlier and was wide
awake at once. But this time he was more restless than ever and
he thought with despair, "We're unlucky, that's it. We've
never had any luck since we've come here. There's something
you can't put your hands on working to destroy us. Everything
goes steadily against us from bad to worse. We'll never have any
luck. I can feel it. We'll starve before I get a job."

Then he realized that his wife, Marthe, was no longer in the
bed beside him. He looked around the room that seemed so
much larger and so much emptier in that light and he thought,
"What's the matter with Marthe? Is it getting that she can't
sleep?" Sitting up, he peered uneasily into the room's dark
corners. There was a light coming from the kitchenette. As he
got out of bed slowly, with his thick hair standing up straight
all over his head, and reached for his slippers and dressing-
gown, the notion that something mysterious and inexorable was
working to destroy them was so strong in him that he suddenly
wanted to stand in front of his wife and shout in anger, "What
can I do? You tell me something to do. What's the use of me
going out to the streets today. I'm going to sit down here and
wait, day after day." That time when they had first got married
and were secure now seemed such a little far-away forgotten
time.

In his eagerness to make his wife feel the bad luck he felt
within him, he went striding across the room, his old, shapeless

17

slippers flapping on the floor, his dressing-gown only half pulled on, looking in that dim light like someone huge, reckless, and full of sudden savage impulse, who wanted to pound a table and shout. "Marthe, Marthe," he called, "what's the matter with you? Why are you up at this time?"

She came into the room carrying their two-year-old boy. "There's nothing the matter with me," she said. "I got up when I heard Walter crying." She was a small, slim, dark woman with black hair hanging on her shoulders, a thin eager face, and large soft eyes, and as she walked over to the window with the boy she swayed her body as though she were humming to him. The light from the window was now a little stronger. She sat there in her old blue kimono holding the boy tight and feeling his head with her hand.

"What's the matter with him?" George said.

"I don't know. I heard him whimpering, so I got up. His head felt so hot."

"Is there anything I can do?" he said.

"I don't think so."

She seemed so puzzled, so worried and aloof from even the deepest bitterness within him, that George felt impatient, as if it were her fault that the child was sick. For a while he watched her rocking back and forth, making always the same faint humming sound, with the stronger light showing the deep frown on her face, and he couldn't seem to think of the child at all. He wanted to speak with sympathy, but he burst out, "I had to get up because I couldn't go on with my own thoughts. We're unlucky, Marthe. We haven't had a day's luck since we've come to this city. How much longer can this go on before they throw us out on the street? I tell you we never should have come here."

She looked up at him indignantly. He couldn't see the fierceness in her face because her head was against the window light. Twice he walked the length of the room, then he stood beside her, looking down at the street. There was now traffic and an increasing steady hum of motion. He felt chilled and his fingers grasped at the collar of his dressing-gown, pulling it across his chest. "It's cold here, and you can imagine what it'll be like in winter," he said. And when Marthe again did not answer, he said sullenly, "You wanted us to come here. You wanted us to give up what we had and come to a bigger city where there were bigger things ahead. Where we might amount to something because of my fine education and your charming manner. You thought we didn't have enough ambition, didn't you?"

"Why talk about it now, George?"

"I want you to see what's happened to us."

"Say I'm responsible. Say anything you wish."

"All right. I'll tell you what I feel in my bones. Luck is against us. Something far stronger than our two lives is working against us. I was thinking about it when I woke up. I must have been thinking about it all through my sleep."

"We've been unlucky, but we've often had a good time, haven't we?" she said.

"Tell me honestly, have we had a day's luck since we got married?" he said brutally.

"I don't know," she said with her head down. Then she looked up suddenly, almost pleading, but afraid to speak.

The little boy started to whimper and then sat up straight, pushing away the blanket his mother tried to keep around him. When she insisted on covering him, he began to fight and she had a hard time holding him till suddenly he was limp in her arms, looking around the darkened room with the bright wonder that comes in a child's fevered eyes.

George watched Marthe trying to soothe the child. The morning light began to fall on her face, making it seem a little leaner, a little narrower and so dreadfully worried. A few years ago everybody used to speak about her extraordinary smile, about the way the lines around her mouth were shaped for laughter, and they used to say, too, that she had a mysterious, tapering, Florentine face. Once a man had said to George, "I remember clearly the first time I met your wife. I said to

19

myself, 'Who is the lady with that marvellous smile?' "

George was now looking at this face as though it belonged to
a stranger. He could think of nothing but the shape of it. There
were so many angles in that light; it seemed so narrow. "I used
to think it was beautiful. It doesn't look beautiful. Would
anybody say it was beautiful?" he thought, and yet these
thoughts had nothing to do with his love for her.

In some intuitive way she knew that he was no longer
thinking of his bad luck, but was thinking of her, so she said
patiently, "Walter seems to have quite a fever, George." Then
he stopped walking and touched Walter's head, which was very
hot.

"Here, let me hold him a while and you get something," he
said. "Get him some aspirin."

"I'll put it in orange juice, if he'll take it," she said.

"For God's sake, turn on the light, Marthe," he called. "This
ghastly light is getting on my nerves."

He tried talking to his son while Marthe was away. "Hello,
Walter, old boy, what's the matter with you? Look at me, big
boy, say something bright to your old man." But the little boy
shook his head violently, stared vacantly at the wall a moment,
and then tried to bury his face in his father's shoulder. So
George, looking disconsolately around the cold room, felt that
it was more barren than ever.

Marthe returned with the orange juice and the aspirin. They
both began to coax Walter to take it. They pretended to be
drinking it themselves, made ecstatic noises with their tongues
as though it were delicious and kept it up till the boy cried,
"Orange, orange, me too," with an unnatural animation. His
eyes were brilliant. Then he swayed as if his spine were made of
putty and fell back in his mother's arms.

"We'd better get a doctor in a hurry, George," Marthe said.

"Do you think it's that bad?"

"Look at him," she said, laying him on the bed. "I'm sure
he's very sick. You don't want to lose him, do you?" and she

20

stared at Walter, who had closed his eyes and was sleeping.

As Marthe in her fear kept looking up at George, she was fingering her old blue kimono, drawing it tighter around her to keep her warm. The kimono had been of a Japanese pattern adorned with clusters of brilliant flowers sewn in silk. George had given it to her at the time of their marriage; now he stared at it, torn as it was at the arms, with pieces of old padding hanging out at the hem, with the light-coloured lining showing through in many places, and he remembered how, when the kimono was new, Marthe used to make the dark hair across her forehead into bangs, fold her arms across her breasts, with her wrists and hands concealed in the sleeve folds, and go around the room in the bright kimono, taking short, prancing steps, pretending she was a Japanese girl.

The kimono now was ragged and gone; it was gone, he thought, like so many bright dreams and aspirations they had once had in the beginning, like so many fine resolutions he had sworn to accomplish, like so many plans they had made and hopes they had cherished.

"Marthe, in God's name," he said suddenly, "the very first money we get, even if we just have enough to put a little down, you'll have to get a decent dressing-gown. Do you hear?"

She was startled. Looking up at him in bewilderment, she swallowed hard, then turned her eyes down again.

"It's terrible to have to look at you in that thing," he muttered.

After he had spoken in this way he was ashamed, and he was able to see for the first time the wild terrified look on her face as she bent over Walter.

"Why do you look like that?" he asked. "Hasn't he just got a little fever?"

"Did you see the way he held the glass when he took the orange juice?"

"No. I didn't notice."

"His hand trembled. Earlier, when I first went to him, and

gave him a drink I noticed the strange trembling in his hand."

"What does it mean?" he said, awed by the fearful way she was whispering.

"His body seemed limp and he could not sit up either. Last night I was reading about such symptoms in the medical column in the paper. Symptoms like that with a fever are symptoms of infantile paralysis."

"Where's the paper?"

"Over there on the table."

George sat down and began to read the bit of newspaper medical advice very calmly; over and over he read it, very calmly. Marthe had described the symptoms accurately; but in a stupid way he could not get used to the notion that his son might have such a dreadful disease. So he remained there calmly for a long time.

And then he suddenly realized how they had been dogged by bad luck; he realized how surely everything they loved was being destroyed day by day and he jumped up and cried out, "We'll have to get a doctor." And as if he realized to the full what was inevitably impending, he cried out, "You're right, Marthe, he'll die. That child will die. It's the luck that's following us. Then it's over. Everything's over. I tell you I'll curse the day I ever saw the light of the world. I'll curse the day we ever met and ever married. I'll smash everything I can put my hands on in this world."

"George, don't go on like that. You'll bring something dreadful down on us," she whispered in terror.

"What else can happen? What else can happen to us worse than this?"

"Nothing, nothing, but please don't go on saying it, George."

Then they both bent down over Walter and they took turns putting their hands on his head. "What doctor will come to us at this house when we have no money?" he kept muttering. "We'll have to take him to a hospital." They remained kneeling together, silent for a long time, almost afraid to speak.

Marthe said suddenly, "Feel, feel his head. Isn't it a little cooler?"

"What could that be?"

"It might be the aspirin working on him."

So they watched, breathing steadily together while the child's head gradually got cooler. Their breathing and their silence seemed to waken the child, for he opened his eyes and stared at them vaguely. "He must be feeling better," George said. "See the way he's looking at us."

"His head does feel a lot cooler."

"What could have been the matter with him, Marthe?"

"It might have been a chill. Oh, I hope it was only a chill."

"Look at him, if you please. Watch me make the rascal laugh."

With desperate eagerness George rushed over to the table, tore off a sheet of newspaper, folded it into a thin strip about eight inches long and twisted it like a cord. Then he knelt down in front of Walter and cried, "See, see," and thrust the twisted paper under his own nose and held it with his upper lip while he wiggled it up and down. He screwed up his eyes diabolically. He pressed his face close against the boy's.

Laughing, Walter put out his hand. "Let me," he said. So George tried to hold the paper moustache against Walter's lip. But that was no good. Walter pushed the paper away and said, "You, you."

"I think his head is cool now," Marthe said. "Maybe he'll be all right."

She got up and walked away from the bed, over to the window with her head down. Standing up, George went to follow her, but his son shouted tyrannically so he had to kneel down and hold the paper moustache under his nose and say, "Look here, look, Walter."

Marthe was trying to smile as she watched them. She took one deep breath after another, as though she would never succeed in filling her lungs with air. But even while she stood there, she grew troubled. She hesitated, she lowered her head and wanted to say, "One of us will find work of some kind, George," but she was afraid.

"I'll get dressed now," she said quietly, and turned to take off her kimono.

As she took off the kimono and was holding it on her arm, her face grew full of deep concern. She held the kimono up so the light shone on the gay silken flowers. Sitting down in the chair, she spread the faded silk on her knee and looked across the room at her sewing basket which was on the dresser by the mirror. She fumbled patiently with the lining, patting the places that were torn; and suddenly she was sure she could draw the torn parts together and make it look bright and new.

"I think I can fix it up so it'll look fine, George," she said.

"Eh," he said. "What are you bothering with that for?" Then he ducked down to the floor again and wiggled his paper moustache fiercely at the child.

IT'S GOOD TO BE HERE
Alden Nowlan

I'm in trouble, she said
to him. That was the first
time in history that anyone
had ever spoken of me.

It was in 1932 when she
was just 14 years old
and men like him
worked all day for
one stinking dollar.

There's quinine, she said.
That's bullshit, he told her.

Then she cried and then
for a long time neither of them
said anything at all and then
their voices kept rising until
they were screaming at each other
and then there was another long silence and then
they began to talk very quietly and at last he said,
Well, I guess we'll just have to make the best of it.

While I lay curled up,
my heart beating,
in the darkness inside her.

OUTCASTS
Arthur S. Bourinot

We are the outcasts
we with the sodden bulging boots
the broken feet
the dirty pack slung on the back
the eyes that dare not meet
our fellows' eyes.

We are the outcasts
we with the hungry empty hearts
the griping pain
the slouching walk the dirty talk
bodies that long have lain
in sodden fields.

We are the outcasts
we of the furtive shifty glance
the whining tone
the canned heat drink the sweaty stink
and food of a dog's soup bone
in the *jungle*.

We are the outcasts
we of the young but grim creased face
battered with grime
the hopeless search the final lurch
and thrust of impetuous crime
to a barren grave.

I AM A TRANSIENT
Henry Paul

I am an unemployed transient; that is to say, I have spent most of the last ten years on the drift. From town to town across the Dominion at least a dozen times and through 40 of the 48 States, by boxcar, blind baggage and highway, I have kept moving. I have alternated periods of unskilled, poorly paid work with living for months at a time on various forms of public relief, or with downright beggary. I am rarely well-dressed and sometimes quite ragged and dirty. I am now 28; I was 18 when I first "hit the road". In point of fact I was graduated directly from a Canadian university into the boxcar.

In December 1929, I was a curiosity, almost a freak. A tramp at that time was a man over 35, semi-illiterate, a beaten hulk of a man with a shady, usually criminal past, and no future. I was a fresh-cheeked, somewhat naive lad with a great faith in what the world held in store for me. Indeed sheer force of physical circumstances alone impelled me to take the first steps. But I was not to remain an exception for long. From towns and villages and farms, and especially from the drought-stricken prairies, new recruits flooded in by the thousands.

Their circumstances showed a strong uniformity. Some were, like me, directly from the classroom; most had been living at home in idleness for a year or two, then had left in disgust or had been shown the door by brutal parents who "had been supporting a family at their age". The inhuman provision of the relief system, which in many places excludes children over a certain age — usually 14 — from the relief check, forced many either to leave home or to take food out of the mouths of younger brothers and sisters. A few left homes to seek adventures, but these were in a decided minority. Most were under 22, some as young as 13 or 14. Virtually none had ever held a decent job or had any work experience; en masse they had no training, trade, or profession to fit them for life in a bitterly competitive world.

Let us consider what happened to these boys — my own case

will do as an example; many others would vary only in particulars. I left home in December, boarded a freight and rode 300 miles in bitterly cold weather. My first stop was at a Canadian town of some 15,000 people, which had, and I believe still has, a large sign somewhere in its environs advertising it as "a friendly city". It was not such to me. Desperately tired and cold after a 15-hour ride in below-zero weather I stumbled down the main street. Naively enough I turned my steps towards the local headquarters of a certain international religious organization which makes quite a display of its social and charitable ideals, and which operates a men's hostel in this town. On my arrival there I asked for a bed. The cutting wind was no colder than the refusal, when the person in charge discovered I lacked the necessary quarter. Then I recalled that one of the "stiffs" who had ridden on the train with me had spoken of sleeping at the police station. I turned thither.

On my arrival I inquired timidly of the sergeant at the desk for a bed. I had a vague idea that I would be given at least a bunk and blankets. The sergeant first took my name, address, and other particulars, then showed me to my "lodgings". Picture to yourself a room about ten feet by ten feet with no ventilation, with rough stone walls and a cement floor, an open water closet in one corner, a girdle of steam pipes all around, a huge globe burning overhead, and absolutely no furniture of any kind. On the floor there already lay sprawled a dozen ragged, unkempt men. They occupied all the available space. To get in at all, I had to step over recumbent bodies. But not even the choking odour of unwashed bodies or the swarms of bed bugs could keep me awake. Space to lie down in there was none, so I slept sitting up. I think I could have slept standing too.

I have slept in many such places since, some very little better, some actually worse, but the memory of that "bed" is still fresh with me. In the morning we were awakened at six. I struggled to my feet; apparently half a dozen more men had come in after I fell asleep. As to where or how they slept, I am not willing to hazard a theory. We filed out of the dungeon and back into the bright freshly-painted offices. The burly sergeant booked us out.

"I want you fellows to get out of town," he snapped. "If I catch any of you guys hanging around here, I'll run you in for thirty days."

The few nearest him nodded meekly and we filed out into the street, for this was no idle threat. I have done a total of 46 days in jail at one time or another for the crime of "being without visible means of support".

The cutting cold tore at me. I did not feel hungry. I had already missed too many meals to feel hungry. But it is possible to feel very, very cold, especially if one's stomach is empty. I was tired too, after the "rest" of the previous night. By a stroke of luck, I turned a corner and ran into one of the "road stiffs" who had come into town on the same freight as I.

This man became my mentor for the next two weeks. If I had not met him, I do not know to what desperate steps I might have been driven. He supplied my initiation into the ways of beggary and vagabondage. I do not care to go into the details, which even at this late stage I find disgusting. It was a difficult job, for I was a delicate, sensitive lad, with a streak of honesty which at first made this life unspeakably hard for me.

As I have said we were together for a scant two weeks. I later learned that my pal had a leg cut off under a freight train, a year afterwards. Sardonically enough he was then "accepted" by the relief office of the municipality in which this occurred. Since that time I have inducted a half-dozen young fellows into the ways of the road. I have found them hungry, bewildered, hopeless. I have rustled them a few meals, broken them into the ropes, then left them. They and I lived miserably, it is true, but by following these methods we were at least able to eat most of the time and generally to get a warm place to sleep.

What is really noteworthy is that these young fellows, like myself, have stayed on the road. I have met them repeatedly in past years, in freights, on the highway, or in flophouses. In fact

I may say here that I have never met or ever heard of anyone who has lived this life for any considerable period of time and has been able to rehabilitate himself completely.

The following spring, when I had been on the road about three months, I got a job. I had almost given up the pretence of looking for work. All winter I had gone through one town after another where I knew no one and no one knew or wanted to know me. I never had time enough to get acquainted before the police ran me out to the next town. While I was in one place my whole time was taken up with the question of how to get food and tobacco and a warm place to sleep. Bitterly cold night-rides on freights, horrible restless "flops", and bad food filled my whole existence. My clothes too had become ragged, marking me as a "stiff" and making me an easy prey for ambitious rookie policemen.

Finally I did get a job, a pick and shovel job at enough to pay for my board, clothes, tobacco, and no more. It was gruelling work for my young untried muscles; but I stuck it out for the six weeks it lasted. I then found myself again "on the bum", again banging back doors, again being looked at askance by snooty employment bureau clerks for having the temerity to ask for a job in a ragged pair of pants. From time to time I got bits of rough, poorly paid work (this was in 1930-31). Always the end was the same. The lay-off, the road again, futility.

There may be persons of sufficient strength of character to live through the combination of filth, misery, and beggary that I have described without becoming to some extent demoralized, but I have not met them. When I first went on the road, there were few men under thirty; today there are many, and they are not newcomers. They are the children of fifteen to twenty who drifted into this life five or ten years back. Those who believe that these youngsters will all come back into life if and when jobs are opened for them do not know the facts. Many are beaten hulks today on whose very faces there is the stamp of enforced beggary and degeneracy.

Do I mean to say that these men are hopelessly lost? Not at all. But they need a definite program of rehabilitation. To reduce the question to whether the men will or will not work is the purest nonsense. As a matter of fact most of them will — for short periods of time — but they have lost all stamina, will, direction. They cannot steer directly towards a long-range ambition. It is this state which I call "boxcar neurosis", as true a neurosis as any in the Freudian canon. They have been hammered out of the form of men and have become worthless both to themselves and to the society around them.

Some highlights of my experiences may be interesting, inasmuch as they illustrate general conditions. Very early in my life on the road I learned to stay away from various religious bodies, which professionally undertake evangelization of the "down and outer". I am not here attacking religion. Most of the friends of the drifter come from the United and Catholic churches. But there are several religious bodies which have established missions, hostels, and the like. The procedure is almost always the same. The group purchases a building on which, of course, they pay no taxes. Then they proceed in the name of charity to jam the building with beds at a concentration of anything up to five times as great as that permitted by law to private rooming-house keepers. After installing a checker board and a handful of last year's magazines as "recreation", they are open for business. The rates are always just a little below what a private rooming-house can profitably charge for the same service. These places are in no sense charitable. Beds are not given away. In each of these places there is a collection of broken down bar-room flies and other seedy types of stiffs, who in return for a bed can be counted on for a testimony to their changed lives when pious contributors are present. To the man on the road, who still retains some self-respect, these "rice-Christians"* are untouchables. In fact to

---

*"Rice-Christians" was originally the name given by white people on the China coast to the hordes of "converts" with which some China missionaries padded their church membership lists. In return for aid given in building a church, or even in return for occasionally attending church, the Chinese "converts" were given two bowls of rice per day. The rice-Christians were, in large part, broken-down opium addicts. Among many of them it was the practice to save a little rice each day with a view to trading it for another pipeful of opium when sufficient rice had been collected.

be called a "mission stiff" is a grave insult.

One great solacer the man on the road has — alcohol. I do not mean to say that all men on the road drink, but the proportion of those who are never sober by choice is perhaps as high as one in four. It is a vicious circle. A man drinks because he is miserable, because he drinks and so on. The difficulty of getting money for drink has led to the use of cheaper substitutes. The two principal ones are rubbing-alcohol and canned heat (the alcohol is squeezed out of the latter through a handkerchief).

Any person who cares to inspect the environs of a hobo camp is reasonably sure to find a number of containers of these liquids scattered around. I do not care to describe here the mental and physical effects of these concoctions. Many of the addicts are hardened reprobates of twenty or so.

Since these men are treated as outcasts, it is only natural that they should become such; they have a kind of closed society with its own conventions, groupings, dignities, and even a partially developed argot of its own. This tendency towards seclusion has been aided by the rapid growth of sexual perversion, made necessary by lack of female companionship. (In ten years I have seen half a dozen women on the road, and these highly unattractive.) Perversions of various types, while by no means universal, are now so common as no longer to be considered marked peculiarities.

As might be expected the physical condition of the men is almost as low as their mental states. Exposure, cold, and hunger have taken their toll. Any scheme for rehabilitation must consider this. A stiff percentage would be unable to do a day's work in their present condition, and would require a long process of rebuilding.

I know I will seem to have painted a very black picture but the problem is a vicious one. I have tried here to state it, not to show how it might be corrected. But certainly the first step to be taken is to stop the flood of new recruits. The number of drifters in Canada today is approaching 150,000. (Not all of them are on the road at the same time, of course.) There are at least three men adrift today for every one in 1929. That is, we have created at least 100,000 tramps or roadstiffs in 10 years. During this decade about 1,000,000 young Canadian boys came to manhood. We have been making a bum out of one young Canadian in every ten.

What is more, this state of affairs has not stopped, neither is it stopping. You are the father or mother of a boy of fourteen. Today there is actually one chance in ten that within a few years he will be picking vermin off himself in a boxcar. If you are a wage worker or farmer, your son's chances are even worse, for it is from the homes of the working class that practically all these boys come — hence the complacency of those in high places.

There is of course only one immediate hope — vigorous governmental action — but how is this to be attained? Those who know the King government's attitude to spending money on social reforms know that unemployment relief will only come through vigorous publicity and agitation; neither the federal nor the provincial governments act progressively on their own initiatives.

The reactionary press in the larger centres maintains a campaign to keep the "bums" on the move; the Canadian imperialists are particularly anxious to get "penniless vagrants" out of sight during the king's visit. On the plea of returning them to homes they haven't got, they are to be banished from the route of the royal itinerary. The Vagrancy Act will no doubt be invoked, as in the past, to herd them into Canadian jails during May and June. A colonial survival of fourteenth-century English feudal legislation against revolting serfs, this Act makes it a jail offense to be "without visible means of support".

The focus of resistance to all this must be the men themselves. A large percentage is at the moment too demoralized to be organizable, but there is a score of transients who have been able to save some tattered remnants of their self-respect. Amongst these I have observed a steadily deepening consciousness of their position and an unwillingness to permit

O ON TO OTTAWA

The Relief Camp Strikers will leave Regina via
C.P.R. Freight

Monday, June 17th
at approx. 10 p.m.

The Federal Government have declared an embargo on our leaving Regina by the same means by which we came.

Only the mass support of Regina Citizens will force the Authorities to keep their hands off us on our way to Ottawa.

We call upon every citizen who supports us in our fight against Forced Slave Labor to assemble at the C.P.R. freight yards between Albert and Broad Street

Monday, June 17th from 10 p.m. until we leave

We extend to Regina Citizens our heartiest thanks for their splendid support in this vital issue.

Publicity Committee.
Relief Camp Strikers.

themselves to be hounded about the country any longer.

When transients in Toronto began mass "tin-canning" this winter they were thrown into jail — but the consequent public interest and sympathy for their plight resulted in their release and in at least some local and temporary relief.

But, as usual, the support of the liberal press has been
sentimental, and more confusing than constructive. "Human
interest" articles, such as appeared in the *Toronto Star*, have
represented the mass of the transients as a fine virile Canadian
young manhood in need only of some temporary assistance in
the way of snow-shovelling or a more elegant but still
temporary flop-house. Such propaganda may have all the best
intentions but it does not face the facts nor strike at the root of
the problem.

What the single unemployed need is not jail and the bum's
rush on the one hand, nor mere winter hand-outs on the other.
They need work and wages. Moreover the hours and the nature
of the work must be adjusted to the endurance of their
weakened bodies, and the wages must be high enough so that
they can build up physical and moral and mental stamina once

more. Nor will this be possible unless the work is of a socially necessary kind. Unemployed camps of the type attempted in the past, and hinted at again by the Leadership League, are simply serf-labour camps to keep the unemployed away from the big centres where he can make his miseries known, and to put him under military control. In this way he is deprived of what democratic rights he has left and turned into a piece of war-material awaiting export to the next world slaughter.

Any effective program for the transient, as for the unemployed in general, must aim at his absorption into normal and useful industry. Initial measures must include immediate and adequate cash relief, clinical and hospital attention, and work-training schools. A federal program of constructive public works must then be created which will provide jobs at union rates. The money can be found; it is being found instead for "military defence". Why also should it not be possible, in a country where thousands lack proper food and shelter, for the government to take over idle factories and finance and train unemployed to run them co-operatively? Why can there not be a national housing program, and schools to make carpenters out of useless transients?

Such a method of approach, if coupled always with the demand for trade-union rates, is the only way to arouse the indifferent trade-unions to the realization that their interests and those of the unemployed are ultimately the same. The worker of today is the transient of tomorrow. In the meantime the unemployed must, of course, build his own independent organization on a militant basis; but he must have the support of the trade-unions, he must feel the solidarity of the working-class movement behind him, if his problem is to be solved.

TWO THIEVES
Kenneth Leslie

I saw him glide through my granary door
on the side of his heel,
and I followed him fair.
It was noon from the haying
and the sun overhead
flamed.

In the feed-bin I caught him
headlong in theft,
unaware
that I stood watching him steal.

And I thought of his need
and I thought of my store
and I turned and left
in haste lest he catch me there;
for I was ashamed.

HORSES OF THE NIGHT
Margaret Laurence

I never knew I had distant cousins who lived up north, until
Chris came down to Manawaka to go to high school. My
mother said he belonged to a large family, relatives of ours, who
lived at Shallow Creek, up north. I was six, and Shallow Creek
seemed immeasurably far, part of a legendary winter country
where no leaves grow and where the breath of seals and polar
bears snuffled out steamily and turned to ice.

"Could plain people live there?" I asked my mother, meaning
people who were not Eskimos. "Could there be a farm?"

"How do you mean?" she said, puzzled. "I told you. That's
where they live. On the farm. Uncle Wilf — that was Chris's
father, who died a few years back — he got the place as a
homestead, donkey's years ago."

"But how could they grow anything? I thought you said it
was up north."

"Mercy," my mother said, laughing, "it's not *that* far north,
Vanessa. It's about a hundred miles beyond Galloping
Mountain. You be nice to Chris, now, won't you? And don't go
asking him a whole lot of questions the minute he steps inside
the door."

How little my mother knew of me, I thought. Chris had
been fifteen. He could be expected to feel only scorn towards
me. I detested the fact that I was so young. I did not think I
would be able to say anything at all to him.

"What if I don't like him?"

"What if you don't?" my mother responded sharply. "You're
to watch your manners, and no acting up, understand? It's
going to be quite difficult enough without that."

"Why does he have to come here, anyway?" I demanded
crossly. "Why can't he go to school where he lives?"

"Because there isn't any high school up there," my mother
said. "I hope he gets on well here, and isn't too homesick.
Three years is a long time. It's very good of your grandfather to
let him stay at the Brick House."

She said this last accusingly, as though she suspected I might
be thinking differently. But I had not thought of it one way or
another. We were all having dinner at the Brick House because

of Chris's arrival. It was the end of August, and sweltering. My grandfather's house looked huge and cool from the outside, the high low-sweeping spruce trees shutting out the sun with their dusky out-fanned branches. But inside it wasn't cool at all. The woodstove in the kitchen was going full blast, and the whole place smelled of roasting meat.

Grandmother Connor was wearing a large mauve apron. I thought it was a nicer colour than the dark bottle-green of her dress, but she believed in wearing sombre shades lest the spirit give way to vanity, which in her case was certainly not much of a risk. The apron came up over her shapeless bosom and obscured part of her cameo brooch, the only jewellery she ever wore, with its portrait of a fiercely bearded man whom I imagined to be either Moses or God.

"Isn't it nearly time for them to be getting here, Beth?" Grandmother Connor asked.

"Train's not due until six," my mother said. "It's barely five-thirty, now. Has Father gone to the station already?"

"He went an hour ago," my grandmother said.

"He would," my mother commented.

"Now, now, Beth," my grandmother cautioned and soothed.

At last the front screen door was hurled open and Grandfather Connor strode into the house, followed by a tall lanky boy. Chris was wearing a white shirt, a tie, grey trousers. I thought, unwillingly, that he looked handsome. His face was angular, the bones showing through the brown skin. His grey eyes were slightly slanted, and his hair was the colour of couchgrass at the end of summer when it has been bleached to a light yellow by the sun. I had not planned to like him, not even a little, but somehow I wanted to defend him when I heard what my mother whispered to my grandmother before they went into the front hall.

"Heavens, look at the shirt and trousers — must've been his father's, the poor kid."

I shot out into the hall ahead of my mother, and then stopped and stood there.

"Hi, Vanessa," Chris said.

"How come you knew who I was?" I asked.

"Well, I knew your mother and dad only had one of a family, so I figured you must be her," he replied, grinning.

The way he spoke did not make me feel I had blundered. My mother greeted him warmly but shyly. Not knowing if she were expected to kiss him or to shake hands, she finally did neither. Grandmother Connor, however, had no doubts. She kissed him on both cheeks and then held him at arm's length to have a proper look at him.

"Bless the child," she said.

Coming from anyone else, this remark would have sounded ridiculous, especially as Chris was at least a head taller. My grandmother was the only person I have ever known who could say such things without appearing false.

"I'll show you your room, Chris," my mother offered.

Grandfather Connor, who had been standing in the living room doorway in absolute silence, looking as granite as a statue in the cemetery, now followed Grandmother out to the kitchen.

"Train was forty minutes late," he said weightily.

"What a shame," my grandmother said. "But I thought it wasn't due until six, Timothy."

"Six!" my grandfather cried. "That's the mainline train. The local's due at five-twenty."

This was not correct, as both my grandmother and I knew. But neither of us contradicted him.

"What on earth are you cooking a roast for, on a night like this?" my grandfather went on. "A person could fry an egg on the sidewalk, it's that hot. Potato salad would've gone down well."

Privately I agreed with this opinion, but I could never permit myself to acknowledge agreement with him on anything. I automatically and emotionally sided with Grandmother in all issues, not because she was inevitably right but because I loved her.

"It's not a roast," my grandmother said mildly. "It's

40

mock-duck. The stove's only been going for an hour. I thought the boy would be hungry after the trip."

My mother and Chris had come downstairs and were now in the living room. I could hear them there, talking awkwardly, with pauses.

"Potato salad," my grandfather declaimed, "would've been plenty good enough. He'd have been lucky to get it, if you ask me anything. Wilf's family hasn't got two cents to rub together. It's me that's paying for the boy's keep."

The thought of Chris in the living room, and my mother unable to explain, was too much for me. I sidled over to the kitchen door, intending to close it. But my grandmother stopped me.

"No," she said, with unexpected firmness. "Leave it open, Vanessa."

I could hardly believe it. Surely she couldn't want Chris to hear? She herself was always able to move with equanimity through a hurricane because she believed that a mighty fortress was her God. But the rest of us were not like that, and usually she did her best to protect us. At the time I felt only bewilderment. I think now that she must have realised Chris would have to learn the Brick House sooner or later, and he might as well start right away.

I had to go into the living room. I had to know how Chris would take my grandfather. Would he, as I hoped, be angry and perhaps even speak out? Or would he, meekly, only be embarrassed?

"Wilf wasn't much good, even as a young man," Grandfather Connor was trumpeting. "Nobody but a simpleton would've taken up a homestead in a place like that. Anybody could've told him that land's no use for a thing except hay."

Was he going to remind us again how well he had done in the hardware business? Nobody had ever given him a hand, he used to tell me. I am sure he believed that this was true. Perhaps it even was true.

"If the boy takes after his father, it's a poor lookout for him," my grandfather continued.

I felt the old rage of helplessness. But as for Chris — he gave no sign of feeling anything. He was sitting on the big wing-backed sofa that curled into the bay window like a black and giant seashell. He began to talk to me, quite easily, just as though he had not heard a word my grandfather was saying.

This method proved to be the one Chris always used in any dealings with my grandfather. When the bludgeoning words came, which was often, Chris never seemed, like myself, to be holding back with a terrible strained force for fear of letting go and speaking out and having the known world unimaginably fall to pieces. He would not argue or defend himself, but he did not apologise, either. He simply appeared to be absent, elsewhere. Fortunately there was very little need for response, for when Grandfather Connor pointed out your shortcomings, you were not expected to reply.

But this aspect of Chris was one which I noticed only vaguely at the time. What won me was that he would talk to me and wisecrack as though I were his same age. He was — although I didn't know the phrase then — a respecter of persons.

On the rare evenings when my parents went out, Chris would come over to mind me. These were the best times, for often when he was supposed to be doing his homework, he would make fantastic objects for my amusement, or his own — pipecleaners twisted into the shape of wildly prancing midget men, or an old set of Christmas-tree lights fixed onto a puppet theatre with a red velvet curtain that really pulled. He had skill in making miniature things of all kinds. Once for my birthday he gave me a leather saddle no bigger than a matchbox, which he had sewn himself, complete in every detail, stirrups and horn, with the criss-cross lines that were the brand name of his ranch, he said, explaining it was a reference to his own name.

"Can I go to Shallow Creek sometime?" I asked one evening.

"Sure. Some summer holidays, maybe. I've got a sister about your age. The others are all grownup."

I did not want to hear. His sisters — for Chris was the only boy — did not exist for me, not even as photographs, because I did not want them to exist. I wanted him to belong only here. Shallow Creek existed, though, no longer filled with ice mountains in my mind but as some beckoning country beyond all ordinary considerations.

"Tell me what it's like there, Chris."

"My gosh, Vanessa, I've told you before, about a thousand times."

"You never told me what your house is like."

"Didn't I? Oh well — it's made out of trees grown right there beside the lake."

"Made out of trees? Gee. Really?"

I could see it. The trees were still growing, and the leaves were firmly and greenly on them. The branches had been coaxed into formations of towers and high-up nests where you could look out and see for a hundred miles or more.

"That lake, you know," Chris said. "It's more like an inland sea. It goes on for ever and ever amen, that's how it looks. And you know what? Millions of years ago, before there were any human beings at all, that lake was full of water monsters. All different kinds of dinosaurs. Then they all died off. Nobody knows for sure why. Imagine them — all those huge creatures, with necks like snakes, and some of them had hackles on their heads, like a rooster's comb only very tough, like hard leather. Some guys from Winnipeg came up a few years back, there, and dug up dinosaur bones, and they found footprints in the rocks."

"Footprints in the *rocks*?"

"The rocks were mud, see, when the dinosaurs went trampling through, but after trillions of years the mud turned into stone and there were these mighty footprints with the claws still showing. Amazing, eh?"

I could only nod, fascinated and horrified. Imagine going swimming in those waters. What if one of the creatures had lived on?

"Tell me about the horses," I said.

"Oh, them. Well, we've got these two riding horses. Duchess and Firefly. I raised them, and you should see them. Really sleek, know what I mean? I bet I could make racers out of them."

He missed the horses, I thought with selfish satisfaction, more than he missed his family. I could visualize the pair, one sorrel and one black, swifting through all the meadows of summer.

"When can I go, Chris?"

"Well, we'll have to see. After I get through high school, I won't be at Shallow Creek much."

"Why not?"

"Because," Chris said, "what I am going to be is an engineer, civil engineer. You ever seen a really big bridge, Vanessa? Well, I haven't either, but I've seen pictures. You take the Golden Gate Bridge in San Francisco, now. Terrifically high — all those thin ribs of steel, joined together to go across this very wide stretch of water. It doesn't seem possible, but it's there. That's what engineers do. Imagine doing something like that, eh?"

I could not imagine it. It was beyond me.

"Where will you go?" I asked. I did not want to think of his going anywhere.

"Winnipeg, to college," he said with assurance.

The Depression did not get better, as everyone had been saying it would. It got worse, and so did the drought. That part of the prairies where we lived was never dustbowl country. The farms around Manawaka never had a total crop failure, and afterwards, when the drought was over, people used to remark on this fact proudly, as though it had been due to some virtue or special status, like the Children of Israel being afflicted by Jehovah but never in real danger of annihilation. But although Manawaka never knew the worst, what it knew was bad enough. Or so I learned later. At the time I saw none of it. For me, the Depression and drought were external and abstract, malevolent gods whose names I secretly learned although they were concealed from me, and whose evil I sensed only

44

superstitiously, knowing they threatened us but not how or why. What I really saw was only what went on in our family.

"He's done quite well all through, despite everything," my mother said. She sighed, and I knew she was talking about Chris.

"I know," my father said. "We've been over all this before, Beth. But quite good just isn't good enough. Even supposing he managed to get a scholarship, which isn't likely, it's only tuition and books. What about room and board? Who's going to pay for that? Your father?"

"I see I shouldn't have brought up the subject at all," my mother said in an aloof voice.

"I'm sorry," my father said impatiently. "But you know, yourself, he's the only one who might possibly —"

"I can't bring myself to ask Father about it, Ewen. I simply cannot do it."

"There wouldn't be much point in asking," my father said, "when the answer is a foregone conclusion. He feels he's done his share, and actually, you know, Beth, he has, too. Three years, after all. He may not have done it gracefully, but he's done it."

We were sitting in the living room, and it was evening. My father was slouched in the grey armchair that was always his. My mother was slenderly straight-backed in the blue chair in which nobody else ever sat. I was sitting on the footstool, beige needlepoint with mathematical roses, to which I had staked my own claim. This seating arrangement was obscurely satisfactory to me, perhaps because predictable, like the three bears. I was pretending to be colouring into a scribbler on my knee, and from time to time my lethargic purple crayon added a feather to an outlandish swan. To speak would be to invite dismissal. But their words forced questions in my head.

"Chris isn't going away, is he?"

My mother swooped, shocked at her own neglect.

"My heavens — are you still up, Vanessa? What am I thinking of?"

"Where is Chris going?"

"We're not sure yet," my mother evaded, chivvying me up the stairs. "We'll see."

He would not go, I thought. Something would happen, miraculously, to prevent him. He would remain, with his long loping walk and his half-slanted grey eyes and his talk that never excluded me. He would stay right here. And soon, because I desperately wanted to, and because every day mercifully made me older, quite soon I would be able to reply with such a lightning burst of knowingness that it would astound him, when he spoke of the space or was it some black sky that never ended anywhere beyond this earth. Then I would not be innerly belittled for being unable to figure out what he would best like to hear. At that good and imagined time, I would not any longer be limited. I would not any longer be young.

I was nine when Chris left Manawaka. The day before he was due to go, I knocked on the door of his room in the Brick House.

"Come in," Chris said. "I'm packing. Do you know how to fold socks, Vanessa?"

"Sure. Of course."

"Well, get folding on that bunch there, then."

I had come to say goodbye, but I did not want to say it yet. I got to work on the socks. I did not intend to speak about the matter of college, but the knowledge that I must not speak about it made me uneasy. I was afraid I would blurt out a reference to it in my anxiety not to. My mother had said, "He's taken it amazingly well — he doesn't even mention it, so we mustn't either."

"Tomorrow night you'll be in Shallow Creek," I ventured.

"Yeh." He did not look up. He went on stuffing clothes and books into his suitcase.

"I bet you'll be glad to see the horses, eh?" I wanted him to say he didn't care about the horses any more and that he would rather stay here.

"It'll be good to see them again," Chris said. "Mind handing over those socks now, Vanessa? I think I can just squash them in at the side here. Thanks. Hey, look at that, will you? Everything's in. Am I an expert packer or am I an expert packer?"

I sat on his suitcase for him so it would close, and then he tied a piece of rope around it because the lock wouldn't lock.

"Ever thought what it would be like to be a traveller, Vanessa?" he asked.

I thought of Richard Halliburton, taking an elephant over the Alps and swimming illicitly in the Taj Mahal lily pool by moonlight.

"It would be keen," I said, because this was the word Chris used to describe the best possible. "That's what I'm going to do someday."

He did not say, as for a moment I feared he might, that girls could not be travellers.

"Why not?" he said. "Sure you will, if you really want to. I got this theory, see, that anybody can do anything at all, anything, if they really set their minds to it. But you have to have this total concentration. You have to focus on it with your whole mental powers, and not let it slip away by forgetting to hold it in your mind. If you hold it in your mind, like, then it's real, see? You take most people, now. They can't concentrate worth a darn."

"Do you think I can?" I enquired eagerly, believing that this was what he was talking about.

"What?" he said. "Oh — sure. Sure I think you can. Naturally."

Chris did not write after he left Manawaka. About a month later we had a letter from his mother. He was not at Shallow Creek. He had not gone back. He had got off the northbound train at the first stop after Manawaka, cashed in his ticket, and thumbed a lift with a truck to Winnipeg. He had written to his mother from there, but had given no address. She had not heard from him since. My mother read Aunt Tess's letter aloud to my father. She was too upset to care whether I was listening or not.

"I can't think what possessed him, Ewen. He never seemed irresponsible. What if something should happen to him? What if he's broke? What do you think we should do?"

"What can we do? He's nearly eighteen. What he does is his business. Simmer down, Beth, and let's decide what we're going to tell your father."

"Oh Lord," my mother said. "There's that to consider, of course."

I went out without either of them noticing. I walked to the hill at the edge of the town, and down into the valley where the scrub oak and poplar grew almost to the banks of the Wachakwa River. I found the oak where we had gone last autumn, in a gang, to smoke cigarettes made of dried leaves and pieces of newspaper. I climbed to the lowest branch and stayed there for a while.

I was not consciously thinking about Chris. I was not thinking of anything. But when at last I cried, I felt relieved afterwards and could go home again.

Chris departed from my mind, after that, with a quickness that was due to the other things that happened. My Aunt Edna, who was a secretary in Winnipeg, returned to Manawaka to live because the insurance company cut down on staff and she could not find another job. I was intensely excited and jubilant about her return, and could not see why my mother seemed the opposite, even though she was as fond of Aunt Edna as I was. Then my brother Roderick was born, and that same year Grandmother Connor died. The strangeness, the unbelievability, of both these events took up all of me.

When I was eleven, almost two years after Chris had left, he came back without warning. I came home from school and found him sitting in our living room. I could not accept that I had nearly forgotten him until this instant. Now that he was present, and real again, I felt I had betrayed him by not thinking of him more.

He was wearing a navy-blue serge suit. I was old enough now to notice that it was a cheap one and had been worn a considerable time. Otherwise, he looked the same, the same smile, the same knife-boned face with no flesh to speak of, the same unresting eyes.

"How come you're here?" I cried. "Where have you been, Chris?"

"I'm a traveller," he said. "Remember?"

He was a traveller all right. One meaning of the word *traveller*, in our part of the world, was a travelling salesman. Chris was selling vacuum cleaners. That evening he brought out his line and showed us. He went through his spiel for our benefit, so we could hear how it sounded.

"Now look, Beth," he said, turning the appliance on and speaking loudly above its moaning roar, "see how it brightens up this old rug of yours? Keen, eh?"

"Wonderful," my mother laughed. "Only we can't afford one."

"Oh well —" Chris said quickly, "I'm not trying to sell one to you. I'm only showing you. Listen, I've only been in this job a month, but I figure this is really a going thing. I mean, it's obvious, isn't it? You take all those old wire carpet-beaters of yours, Beth. You could kill yourself over them and your carpet isn't going to look one-tenth as good as it does with this."

"Look, I don't want to seem —" my father put in, "but, hell, they're not exactly a new invention, and we're not the only ones who can't afford —"

"This is a pretty big outfit, you know?" Chris insisted. "Listen, I don't plan to stay, Ewen. But a guy could work at it for a year or so, and save — right? Lots of guys work their way through university like that."

I needed to say something really penetrating, something that would show him I knew the passionate truth of his conviction.

"I bet —" I said, "I bet you'll sell a thousand, Chris."

Two years ago, this statement would have seemed self-evident, unquestionable. Yet now, when I had spoken, I knew that I did not believe it.

The next time Chris visited Manawaka, he was selling

magazines. He had the statistics worked out. If every sixth person in town would get a subscription to *Country Guide*, he could make a hundred dollars in a month. We didn't learn how he got on. He didn't stay in Manawaka a full month. When he turned up again, it was winter. Aunt Edna phoned.

"Nessa? Listen, kiddo, tell your mother she's to come down if it's humanly possible. Chris is here, and Father's having fits."

So in five minutes we were scurrying through the snow, my mother and I, with our overshoes not even properly done up and our feet getting wet. He need not have worried. By the time we reached the Brick House, Grandfather Connor had retired to the basement, where he sat in the rocking chair beside the furnace, making occasional black pronouncements like a subterranean oracle. These loud utterances made my mother and aunt wince, but Chris didn't seem to notice any more than he ever had. He was engrossed in telling us about the mechanism he was holding. It had a cranker handle like an old-fashioned sewing machine.

"You attach the ball of wool here, see? Then you set this little switch here, and adjust this lever, and you're away to the races. Neat, eh?"

It was a knitting machine. Chris showed us the finished products. The men's socks he had made were coarse wool, one pair in grey heather and another in maroon. I was impressed.

"Gee — can I do it, Chris?"

"Sure. Look, you just grab hold of the handle right here."

"Where did you get it?" my mother asked.

"I've rented it. The way I figure it, Beth, I can sell these things at about half the price you'd pay in a store, and they're better quality."

"Who are you going to sell them to?" Aunt Edna enquired.

"You take all these guys who do outside work — they need heavy socks all year round, not just in winter. I think this thing could be quite a gold mine."

"Before I forget," my mother said, "how's your mother and the family keeping?"

"They're okay," Chris said in a restrained voice. "They're not short of hands, if that's what you mean, Beth. My sisters have their husbands there."

Then he grinned, casting away the previous moment, and dug into his suitcase.

"Hey, I haven't shown you — these are for you, Vanessa, and this pair is for Roddie."

My socks were cherry-coloured. The very small ones for my brother were turquoise.

Chris only stayed until after dinner, and then he went away again.

After my father died, the whole order of life was torn. Nothing was known or predictable any longer. For months I lived almost entirely within myself, so when my mother told me one day that Chris couldn't find any work at all because there were no jobs and so he had gone back to Shallow Creek to stay, it made scarcely any impression on me. But that summer, my mother decided I ought to go away for a holiday. She hoped it might take my mind off my father's death. What, if anything, was going to take her mind off his death, she did not say.

"Would you like to go to Shallow Creek for a week or so?" she asked me. "I could write to Chris's mother."

Then I remembered, all in a torrent, the way I had imagined it once, when he used to tell me about it — the house fashioned of living trees, the lake like a sea where monsters had dwelt, the grass that shone like green wavering light while the horses flew in the splendour of their pride.

"Yes," I said. "Write to her."

The railway did not go through Shallow Creek, but Chris met me at Challoner's Crossing. He looked different, not only thinner, but — what was it? Then I saw that it was the fact that his face and neck were tanned red-brown, and he was wearing denims, farm pants, and a blue plaid shirt open at the neck. I liked him like this. Perhaps the change was not so much in him as in myself, now that I was thirteen. He looked masculine in a way I had not been aware of, before.

"C'mon, kid," he said. "The limousine's over here."

It was a wagon and two horses, which was what I had expected, but the nature of each was not what I had expected. The wagon was a long and clumsy one, made of heavy planking, and the horses were both plough horses, thick in the legs, and badly matched as a team. The mare was short and stout, matronly. The gelding was very tall and gaunt, and he limped.

"Allow me to introduce you," Chris said. "Floss — Trooper — this is Vanessa."

He did not mention the other horses, Duchess and Firefly, and neither did I, not all the fortnight I was there. I guess I had known for some years now, without realising it, that the pair had only ever existed in some other dimension.

Shallow Creek wasn't a town. It was merely a name on a map. There was a grade school a few miles away, but that was all. They had to go to Challoner's Crossing for their groceries. We reached the farm, and Chris steered me through the crowd of aimless cows and wolfish dogs in the yard, while I flinched with panic.

It was perfectly true that the house was made out of trees. It was a fair-sized but elderly shack, made out of poplar poles and chinked with mud. There was an upstairs, which was not so usual around here, with three bedrooms, one of which I was to share with Chris's sister, Jeannie, who was slightly younger than I, a pallid-eyed girl who was either too shy to talk or who had nothing to say. I never discovered which, because I was so reticent with her myself, wanting to push her away, not to recognise her, and at the same time experiencing a shocked remorse at my own unacceptable feelings.

Aunt Tess, Chris's mother, was severe in manner and yet wanting to be kind, worrying over it, making tentative overtures which were either ignored or repelled by her older daughters and their monosyllabic husbands. Youngsters swam in and out of the house like shoals of nameless fishes. I could not see how so many people could live here, under the one roof, but then I learned they didn't. The married daughters had their own dwelling places, nearby, but some kind of communal life was maintained. They wrangled endlessly but they never left one another alone, not even for a day.

Chris took no part at all, none. When he spoke, it was usually to the children, and they would often follow him around the yard or to the barn, not pestering but just trailing along in clusters of three or four. He never told them to go away. I liked him for this, but it bothered me, too. I wished he would return his sisters' bickering for once, or tell them to clear out, or even yell at one of the kids. But he never did. He closed himself off from squabbling voices just as he used to do with Grandfather Connor's spearing words.

The house had no screens on the doors or windows, and at meal times the flies were so numerous you could hardly see the food for the iridescent-winged blue-black bodies squirming all over it. Nobody noticed my squeamishness except Chris, and he was the only one from whom I really wanted to conceal it.

"Fan with your hand," he murmured.

"It's okay," I said quickly.

For the first time in all the years we had known each other, we could not look the other in the eye. Around the table, the children stabbed and snivelled, until Chris's oldest sister, driven frantic, shrieked, *Shut up shut up shut up.* Chris began asking me about Manawaka then, as though nothing were going on around him.

They were due to begin haying, and Chris announced that he was going to camp out in the bluff near the hayfields. To save himself the long drive in the wagon each morning, he explained, but I felt this wasn't the real reason.

"Can I go, too?" I begged. I could not bear the thought of living in the house with all the others who were not known to me, and Chris not here.

"Well, I don't know —"

"Please. Please, Chris. I won't be any trouble. I promise."

Finally he agreed. We drove out in the big hayrack, its slatted sides rattling, its old wheels jolting metallically. The road was narrow and dirt, and around it the low bushes grew, wild rose and blueberry and wolf willow with silver leaves. Sometimes we would come to a bluff of pale-leaved poplar trees, and once a red-winged blackbird flew up out of the branches and into the hot dusty blue of the sky.

Then we were there. The hayfields lay beside the lake. It was my first view of the water which had spawned saurian giants so long ago. Chris drove the hayrack through the fields of high coarse grass and on down almost to the lake's edge, where there was no shore but only the green rushes like floating meadows in which the water birds nested. Beyond the undulating reeds the open lake stretched, deep, green-grey, out and out, beyond sight.

No human word could be applied. The lake was not lonely or untamed. These words relate to people, and there was nothing of people here. There was no feeling about the place. It existed in some world in which man was not yet born. I looked at the grey reaches of it and felt threatened. It was like the view of God which I had held since my father's death. Distant, indestructible, totally indifferent.

Chris had jumped down off the hayrack.

"We're not going to camp *here*, are we?" I asked and pleaded.

"No. I just want to let the horses drink. We'll camp up there in the bluff."

I looked. "It's still pretty close to the lake, isn't it?"

"Don't worry," Chris said, laughing. "You won't get your feet wet."

"I didn't mean that."

Chris looked at me.

"I know you didn't," he said. "But let's learn to be a little tougher, and not let on, eh? It's necessary."

Chris worked through the hours of sun, while I lay on the half-formed stack of hay and looked up at the sky. The blue air trembled and spun with the heat haze, and the hay on which I was lying held the scents of grass and dust and wild mint.

In the evening, Chris took the horses to the lake again, and then he drove the hayrack to the edge of the bluff and we spread out our blankets underneath it. He made a fire and we had coffee and a tin of stew, and then we went to bed. We did not wash, and we slept in our clothes. It was only when I was curled up uncomfortably with the itching blanket around me that I felt a sense of unfamiliarity at being here, with Chris only three feet away, a self-consciousness I would not have felt even the year before. I do not think he felt this sexual strangeness. If he wanted me not to be a child — and he did — it was not with the wish that I would be a woman. It was something else.

"Are you asleep, Vanessa?" he asked.

"No. I think I'm lying on a tree root."

"Well, shift yourself, then," he said. "Listen, kid, I never said anything before, because I didn't really know what to say, but — you know how I felt about your dad dying, and that, don't you?"

"Yes," I said chokingly. "It's okay. I know."

"I used to talk with Ewen sometimes. He didn't see what I was driving at, mostly, but he'd always listen, you know? You don't find many guys like that."

We were both silent for a while.

"Look," Chris said finally. "Ever noticed how much brighter the stars are when you're completely away from any houses? Even the lamps up at the farm, there, make enough of a glow to keep you from seeing properly like you can out here. What do they make you think about, Vanessa?"

"Well —"

"I guess most people don't give them much thought at all, except maybe to say — *very pretty* — or like that. But the point is, they aren't like that. The stars and planets, in themselves, are just not like that, not *pretty*, for heaven's sake. They're gigantic — some of them burning — imagine those worlds tearing through space and made of pure fire. Or the ones that are absolutely dead — just rock or ice and no warmth in them. There must be some, though, that have living creatures. You wonder what *they* could look like, and what they feel. We won't ever get to know. But somebody will know, someday. I really believe that. Do you ever think about this kind of thing at all?"

He was twenty-one. The distance between us was still too great. For years I had wanted to be older so I might talk with him, but now I felt unready.

"Sometimes," I said, hesitantly, making it sound like *Never.*

"People usually say there must be a God," Chris went on, "because otherwise how did the universe get here? But that's ridiculous. If the stars and planets go on to infinity, they could have existed forever, for no reason at all. Maybe they weren't ever created. Look — what's the alternative? To believe in a God who is brutal. What else could He be? You've only got to look anywhere around you. It would be an insult to Him to believe in a God like that. Most people don't like talking about this kind of thing — it embarrasses them, you know? Or else they're not interested. I don't mind. I can always think about things myself. You don't actually need anyone to talk to. But about God, though — if there's a war, like it looks there will be, would people claim that was planned? What kind of a God would pull a trick like that? And yet, you know, plenty of guys would think it was a godsend, and who's to say they're wrong? It would be a job, and you'd get around and see places."

He paused, as though waiting for me to say something. When I did not, he resumed.

"Ewen told me about the last war, once. He hardly ever talked about it, but this once he told me about seeing the horses sink into the mud, actually going under, you know? And the way their eyes looked when they realised they weren't going to get out. Ever seen horses' eyes when they're afraid, I mean really berserk with fear, like in a bush-fire? Ewen said a guy tended to concentrate on the horses because he didn't dare think what was happening to the men. Including himself. Do you ever listen to the news at all, Vanessa?"

"I—"

I could only feel how foolish I must sound, still unable to reply as I would have wanted, comprehendingly. I felt I had failed myself utterly. I could not speak even the things I knew. As for the other things, the things I did not know, I resented Chris's facing me with them. I took refuge in pretending to be asleep, and after a while Chris stopped talking.

Chris left Shallow Creek some months after the war began, and joined the Army. After his basic training he was sent to England. We did not hear from him until about a year later, when a letter arrived for me.

"Vanessa — what's wrong?" my mother asked.

"Nothing."

"Don't fib," she said firmly. "What did Chris say in his letter, honey?"

"Oh — not much."

She gave me a curious look and then she went away. She would never have demanded to see the letter. I did not show it to her and she did not ask about it again.

Six months later my mother heard from Aunt Tess. Chris had been sent home from England and discharged from the Army because of a mental breakdown. He was now in the provincial mental hospital and they did not know how long he would have to remain there. He had been violent, before, but now he was not violent. He was, the doctors had told his mother, passive.

Violent. I could not associate the word with Chris, who had been so much the reverse. I could not bear to consider what anguish must have catapulted him into that even greater anguish. But the way he was now seemed almost worse. How might he be? Sitting quite still, wearing the hospital's grey dressing-gown, the animation gone from his face?

My mother cared about him a great deal, but her immediate thought was not for him.

"When I think of you, going up to Shallow Creek that time," she said, "and going out camping with him, and what might have happened — "

I, also, was thinking of what might have happened. But we were not thinking of the same thing. For the first time I recognised, at least a little, the dimensions of his need to talk that night. He must have understood perfectly well how impossible it would be, with a thirteen-year-old. But there was no one else. All his life's choices had grown narrower and narrower. He had been forced to return to the alien lake of home, and when finally he saw a means of getting away, it could only be into a turmoil which appalled him and which he dreaded even more than he knew. I had listened to his words, but I had not really heard them, not until now. It would not have made much difference to what happened, but I wished it were not too late to let him know.

Once when I was on holiday from college, my mother got me to help her clean out the attic. We sifted through boxes full of junk, old clothes, schoolbooks, bric-a-brac that once had been treasures. In one of the boxes I found the miniature saddle that Chris had made for me a long time ago.

"Have you heard anything recently?" I asked, ashamed that I had not asked sooner.

She glanced up at me. "Just the same. It's always the same. They don't think there will be much improvement."

Then she turned away.

"He always used to seem so — hopeful. Even when there was really nothing to be hopeful about. That's what I find so strange. He *seemed* hopeful, didn't you think?"

"Maybe it wasn't hope," I said.

"How do you mean?"

I wasn't certain myself. I was thinking of all the schemes he'd had, the ones that couldn't possibly have worked, the unreal solutions to which he'd clung because there were no others, the brave and useless strokes of fantasy against a depression that was both the world's and his own.

"I don't know," I said. "I just think things were always more difficult for him than he let on, that's all. Remember that letter?"

"Yes."

"Well — what it said was that they could force his body to march and even to kill, but what they didn't know was that

he'd fooled them. He didn't live inside it any more."

"Oh Vanessa——" my mother said. "You must have suspected right then."

"Yes, but——"

I could not go on, could not say that the letter seemed only the final heartbreaking extension of that way he'd always had of distancing himself from the absolute unbearability of battle.

I picked up the tiny saddle and turned it over in my hand. "Look. His brand, the name of his ranch. The Criss-Cross."

"What ranch?" my mother said, bewildered.

"The one where he kept his racing horses. Duchess and Firefly."

Some words came into my head, a single line from a poem I had once heard. I knew it referred to a lover who did not want the morning to come, but to me it had another meaning, a different relevance.

Slowly, slowly, horses of the night——

The night must move like this for him, slowly, all through the days and nights. I could not know whether the land he journeyed through was inhabited by terrors, the old monster-kings of the lake, or whether he had discovered at last a way for himself to make the necessary dream perpetual.

I put the saddle away once more, gently and ruthlessly, back into the cardboard box.

TO A GENERATION UNEMPLOYED
Aquarius

In heaven they neither eat nor drink
Nor in the nether world, I think.
Neither are they in marriage given
In hell, 'tis said, nor yet in heaven.
So after four years on the dole,
Though still together, body and soul,
You're equally prepared to grace
The social life of either place.
But what a deal with death is yours
Before you reach the other shores.

Many a lad like you and me
To save the Empire crossed the sea
And fought for right and swallowed lies
In Flanders fields and there he lies.
They died for us; they died in vain.
And soon their sons shall die again.
For hope with their expiring breath
Went out. For us a second death.

So now that peace and plenty reign
Keep out of sight and don't complain.
For though you live on bitter bread,
Though faith and hope are in you dead,
On charity you may rely
So do not in the body die,
For soon the guns begin, and then
There will be certain need of men.

Not yet the writing on the wall
Has specified how you shall fall.
Some fair-haired Prussian thrusting through
(For he is unemployed as you)
May give you peace, or I perhaps
And other well-conditioned chaps —

A loyal guard of volunteers
When Bolshevism's head appears —
Will halt and form a hollow square
And on a gallows hang you there.
So lie and dream your life-in-death
Or stumble on with borrowed breath,
And I'll erect on your behalf
This temporary epitaph:
These at a time when stocks were falling,
An hour when bonds had taken flight,
Forsook their mercenary calling
And walked out blindly in the night.
They ceased to earn, and markets mended;
They starved and spared the budget grief.
We all were brave; ah! they were splendid,
And rescued business — on relief.

PRAIRIE
Anne Marriott

The restless, never-sated pagan wind
Shakes its grey bones across the hungry soil,
Mile after mile — grey mile, green mile —
The empty stubble left from last year's toil,
Summer fallow and few threads of wheat,
Old paintless shanty, cows, a gaunt-ribbed hound . . .
The tinny-brilliant circle of the sky
Like a cookie-cutter slices out a round
Of dusty bareness, centred by a man

Who plods, bent-necked, in tattered overalls;
A dirty-coloured cloud crawls round the west.
(In the next town they're having thundersqualls.)
The old wild greedy wind whirls out the oats,
(No crop this year, not even winter's feed)
While over, over, up and down and over,
Bounces the tumbleweed.

THE GOLDEN AGE OF BOONDOGGLING
James H. Gray

Many millions of dollars were spent on public works in western Canada in the first years of the Bennett administration, but few of us on relief in Winnipeg ever got any of it. Post-offices or federal buildings went up in most of the cities, and Winnipeg obtained a new auditorium. These projects, however, gave work to only a few building tradesmen, and the idea of combating unemployment with a public-works program was an early casualty of the campaign of organized business for balanced budgets and lower taxes.

The closest any of us on relief ever got to socially useful labour was sawing cordwood, but we were drafted periodically for all the make-work projects, like raking leaves, picking rock, digging dandelions, and tidying up back lanes. These "boondoggles", as the Chicago *Tribune* was later to christen them, were devised to enable us to work off the assistance we received, and our services were demanded for a couple of days once a month. It was all justified on the grounds that the exercise would be good for us, that working would improve our morale, and that, by providing us with a token opportunity to work for our relief, we would be freed of the stigma of accepting charity. None of these dubious propositions had much validity. The fatuous nature of the projects the authorities invented quickly brought the entire make-work concept into disrepute.

My first boondoggle assignment came with the first issue of relief I collected. A printed work-slip instructed me to report to the Woodyard foreman to work for three afternoons. The foreman explained the system. There were 4,000 or 5,000 cords of wood in the piles, which extended clear around the yard on four sides. Strung out down the centre of the two- or three-acre courtyard were a dozen saw-horses, or "saw-bucks" as the foreman called them. Beside each saw-horse was stacked half a cord of wood in four-foot lengths. This wood was to be cut into three pieces — stove-lengths. Half the work-gang would saw and the other would load and pile. The pilers would pick up the cut wood and throw it on a heap in front of the saw-horses. One piler would serve two cutters. The rest would help load cordwood onto the horse-drawn sleighs. When the cutters finished their quota, they could go home. Everybody else would stay until 4:30 to load the trucks with cut wood, for the social welfare families, and the sleighs with cordwood, for the unemployed on relief who were supposed to saw it themselves. After my experience with a buck-saw the first afternoon, I never did. We always managed to have seventy-five cents on hand with which to hire a truck-mounted circular saw that followed the wood sleighs around the city.

When the foreman finished his instructions, my instinct was to choose the piling job. Not only had I never held a cordwood saw in my hands, I had never done any manual labour. But I became somehow caught up in the rush for the saws, and almost before I knew it I was headed for a saw-horse with a saw in my hand. This was one of the crowning blunders of my life, a fact that must have been obvious to any half-observant beholder. From any angle, I cut a ludicrous figure as I moved towards the field of combat. I was costumed in a soft felt hat, silk scarf, and form-fitting overcoat with a small velvet collar. I wore light chamois gloves, silk socks, and light oxfords. I could not even carry a buck-saw gracefully, let alone saw with it, but I located a vacant saw-horse and went to work.

How far below zero the temperature was that day, I never knew. I remember only that a cold wind was blowing and there were gusts of snow in the air. The first piece of wood fell from my log, and the second. Soon I was gasping for breath, and my arms started to ache. I tried resting, but that was no good, for the wind fanned the perspiration into ice on my hair.

It was while I was catching my breath that I saw the discarded gasoline-powered circular saws standing in the corner of the yard. Either machine could have sawed as much wood in an afternoon as our entire work-gang. The two machines, in a couple of days, could have cut all the wood the welfare families consumed in a week, perhaps in a month. But they stood idle in silent mockery of our puny efforts as the administrators of unemployment relief repudiated the machine age and set their course back through history in the general direction of the stone age.

My hands and feet were numb with cold before I discovered it was permissible to leave the saw-horses and go into the shack to get warm and have a smoke. Darkness fell, and I was not half through my pile. All the other buckers, save two, had long since finished their stint and departed. At 4:30 I was more dead than alive, and then the foreman unveiled another rule. Those who failed to finish their piles would have to come back the following morning!

"And look, you," he said, meaning me, "when you come back, put on some work clothes. Don't come around here all dressed up like a dude to buck wood!" His disgust was awesome, and I was almost too exhausted to reply.

"These," I said, "*are* my work clothes. I've been going to work all my life in clothes like these. They're the only clothes I have."

"Then for God sake get yourself some rough clothes."

I got mad.

"Look, damn it, if I had money to buy work clothes with, I wouldn't be on relief. And anyway, what clothes I wear is none of your goddam business!"

The other less printable things I said taught me my first lesson in relief deportment — never, under any circumstances, swear at a straw-boss who is ordering you around. He rode me continually the next two days. That foreman's name was the first I put down on my son-of-a-bitch list of men with whom I would some day settle some scores. The list grew and grew during the next couple of years. The day I got a job again I forgot them all.

I completed my wood-sawing assignment the next morning and in the afternoon switched to the piling department. It was no soft touch either, because I picked a couple of men who were obvious experts. They brought their own "Swede-saws" with them, and the first one, clearly a refugee from a lumber camp, was through in little over half an hour. The other was done within an hour. By then I had aches in new places in my back from rapid stooping and lifting and throwing.

The next day, I discovered the age-old dodge of beating straw-bosses. They could not stop you from going to the outdoor privy or into the shack once an hour to get warm. The third afternoon was endurable.

By long odds, the most imaginative boondoggle of them all was the Exhibition Grounds clean-up. Winnipeg once had a summer exhibition on a 100-acre site in the north-west part of the city. There had been a race-track and the usual exhibition buildings, but these were all torn down, or had blown away, after the First World War. The grounds had been vacant ever since, though a section was sometimes used for tourist camping. It was the sort of place that periodically attracted the attention of aldermen, and one summer they decided the time had come for a clean-up. A small army of us went off with a batch of wheelbarrows and picked up all the old tin cans, bottles, shoes, rags, paper, and other junk that had collected on this spot of prairie over twenty years. There was not as much as might have been expected and the pile we collected was perhaps ten feet across and three or four feet high at the crown. Trucks from the engineer's department took the debris to the city dump.

When we arrived on the second day, a supply of shovels, rakes, and picks had been laid in. The foreman distributed them among us and led us over to a corner where he measured off an area about ten feet square. He said he wanted a hole dug three or four feet deep. While we were digging, other men with the wheelbarrows scoured the area for field stones and dumped their loads beside our excavation. Naturally, as we dug, we pondered the nature of our project. The consensus was that we were preparing the foundation for either a tool-shed or a flag-pole. No one came close to guessing the real nature of the project. Before we finished digging, the foreman came over and revised his calculations. We were deep enough, he said. Now we should take the pile of stones that had been gathered and put them in the hole. One fellow needed better direction. How precisely did the foreman want them piled?

"Piled? Piled?" the foreman answered. "Who said anything about piling them? Throw the — stones in the — hole. Then we'll cover them with dirt and scatter the rest of the dirt around on the low spots."

Somebody laughed. Several swore. The foreman exploded:

"All right, all right, come on, let's get to work. This ain't my idea. I don't get paid to think. I get paid to do as I'm told, and this is what I was told to do. Maybe this afternoon, when we run out of rocks, we will just dig two holes and transfer the dirt."

And this was almost what we did. We went around the grounds with shovels and rakes, levelling off imperceptible high spots and scattering the earth into imperceptible low spots.

It was invariably the same on these boondoggles. The foremen in charge seemed to resent the work more than the people who had to do it. It offended their sense of the fitness of things, and they took pains to assure us that what we were about to be employed at was not their idea. They would much rather have been engaged in building something big and permanent and useful. Yet such projects as these at least had the merit of transparency. No one tried to disguise them or make them into anything except what they were — organized time-wasting. There were others, equally useless, that were dressed up to look useful.

Many streets and lanes in the outlying sections of the city needed ditching and grading. This work, however, could only have been done if the cost was charged to the frontage property, and regular employees of the city would have had to do the work for regular wages. The taxpayers would not pay for it, and regular employees would not permit the work to be done by the unemployed. The net result was that the work was not done, and regular employees of the city were laid off and went on relief. Nevertheless, we were put to work digging ditches and grading streets, but deep in the woods where nobody lived.

I worked on a couple of these projects. Surveyors went far out into the bush in south Fort Rouge, hundreds of yards from the nearest house, and farther from sewer and water. A street a couple of blocks long was laid out. We went out first with axes and grubhooks and cleaned off the brush. Then we got picks and shovels and dug ditches. We threw the mud from the ditches onto the road. We levelled the road and graded it with hand tools. The job took relief gangs working in relays all summer in 1932. When we were finished, it was a nice mud road that started nowhere, led nowhere, and, for all I know, still leads nowhere.

The project that probably will be longest remembered by all reliefers as the zaniest ever devised was the great anti-dandelion offensive of the summer of 1931. When I returned to relief, after my discharge from King Edward Hospital, my first work-slip directed me to report to a Parks Board foreman in River Heights. There were several differences between this work-slip and the one given out during the winter. It was for three days instead of the then-normal two, and our grocery allowance was increased by thirty cents. This was to compensate for the extra cost of taking a lunch to work. They had figured it pretty fine. A pint of milk was five cents, and a couple of eggs for sandwiches, with four slices of bread, absorbed the other nickel.

Before we set off for the job the first morning, the foreman stood on a tool-chest and made a little speech.

"Men," he said, "when we leave here we're going to walk over to the top of Niagara Street and start cleaning the dandelions off the boulevards. If everybody will co-operate, we will get along just fine. Nobody expects you to bust a gut on this job, but, if you sort of set yourself some sort of goal, time is bound to go quicker. There is only one rule: You can kneel down, sit down, or lie down, but I don't want you standing up. Standing up will attract the attention of the people on the street, and if they see you standing around doing nothing some of these dames will be phoning in to raise hell. Then I get hell, and if I do I'll dish out some myself!"

We moved in on the dandelions in column of route, armed with a weed-sticker and a waterproof sack on which to kneel. River Heights in Winnipeg is laid out with twelve-foot grass boulevards separating the pavement and the sidewalks. A half-dozen of us lined up on either side of the street and the anti-dandelion offensive was on. It was a beautiful August morning, and the first hours passed quickly. The grass was rather thickly infested with dormant dandelions. We jabbed and pulled and jabbed and pulled. In an hour we travelled about 250 or 300 feet, leaving trails of dandelion-tops behind us. A couple of men were detailed on each side to rake up the harvest and put it in sacks.

Even in boondoggling, individualistic streaks began to emerge. The innately methodical edged ahead of the line. Some would be thorough and spare not the smallest weed. Others would take only the larger weeds and ignore the rest. Still others would work carefully in an effort to get the root out intact. A contest developed to see who could extract the longest root.

We had been working for an hour or so when two fellows on my immediate right got into a squabble. Over what? Over this: John accused Joe of chiselling on his territory. Joe, said John, was covering the narrowest front of anyone in the line. But when he pulled out his dandelions he pushed them over on John's side. This would give the impression to the foreman that John was lead-swinging while Joe was cutting a wide swath. Joe, of course, denied it and said John was crazy. They loudly exchanged insults until the foreman put the width of the street between them.

What did the rest of us do? Laugh at them? We did not. We looked back down the trail of dandelions behind us, and several other arguments of a similar nature broke out. When lunch-time came, the dispute became the subject of lively controversy. I was on John's side — mainly, I suspect, because he seemed a nicer guy than Joe.

"Naw," said another dandelioner, "that John is always pulling something like that. Always arguing with everybody. I've been on work-gangs with him before. Once he was water-boy and belly-ached because we threw half a dipper of water away when we were through drinking. And he wouldn't leave the water in the shade so we could wander over and get a drink. No, the bastard, he had to keep it right on the road where it got hotter than hell and full of dust. Naw, take it from me, that guy John's a screwball."

Weren't we all!

By the time we were at work for an hour after lunch we had squeezed every conceivable blob of interest out of the job. We kneeled and jabbed dandelions, we sat down and jabbed dandelions, we lolled full length and jabbed dandelions. We sharpened the blades of the knives. We swapped experiences. We watched housewives going shopping. Then a band of ten-year-old boys materialized out of nowhere. Some were friendly. Some wanted to show off. Some just stood and stared. Despite the efforts of the foreman to drive them off, they got in our hair. One little fellow was full of questions.

"How much do you get paid? I could do that. Could I get a job?"

I told him we didn't get paid.

This he refused to believe, and he tried to trip me with other questions. That men would go to all the trouble of clearing his boulevard of weeds without getting paid made less sense to him than it did to us. He went off to discuss the mystery with a couple of friends.

"Of course they don't get paid," said one of them. "Don't you know they're all crooks? My mother said they're prisoners from Headingley Jail, and they are working out here now because they got the Parliament Buildings grounds all cleaned up. Prisoners don't get paid, you dope."

"Aw, you're nuts," said another. "I saw those prisoners at the Parliament Buildings and they were all wearing yellow pants."

"G'wan, they weren't either. Some wore blue pants and blue coats, just like those guys over there!" The argument went on and on.

I don't know how the others felt. Perhaps I was feeling sorry for myself, but I was slowly developing an antipathy for small boys. It wasn't their fault that we were on relief and picking dandelions. Yet I looked at these kids and felt a great compulsion to go some place — to the City Hall or the relief office, or the Parliament Buildings — and punch somebody in the nose.

It was just before five o'clock when a dandelioner from the other side of the street exploded. A group of boys had been fooling around. I don't know what touched off the explosion. In any event, he leaped to his feet and, turning to a group of women on a near-by lawn, waved his dandelion sticker menacingly, and shouted:

"Goddamn it, somebody get these little bastards the hell out of here or I'll bury this in their guts!"

The sound of his voice seemed to frighten him. He sat down as quickly as he had risen, shaking and jabbing his knife into the ground, as if to try to dig a hole to crawl into.

The effect of his outburst was instantaneous. The kids were called home and you could see the women in angry discussion. All of us expected there would be trouble, because someone was certain to report us to the relief office. Conceivably, the man might be cut off relief. We agreed to tell whatever lies were necessary to protect him. However, nothing happened as far as we could discover, for the culprit stayed with the gang for the next two days.

On the second day, the heat in the early afternoon was

72

terrific, and it was our bad luck to be working on a street where the trees were young and the shade was sparse. Along about 3:30 we got a pleasant surprise. A young woman came to the foreman, spoke to him for a few minutes, and went back into her house. A half-hour later she called the foreman over. He emerged from the house carrying a large earthen ten-gallon pickle crock containing a block of ice. The woman followed him with a large glass pitcher, full of lemonade that she emptied over the ice, and then she returned to the house. When the lemonade was finished, we took the jar back, rang the bell, and waited, because we did want to thank her. But, though we had heard movement in the house, she did not answer. We left the jar and went back to the dandelions.

The gift of the lemonade itself elevated our spirits far more than a mere cold drink on a hot day ever could have. Perhaps there was a touch of gin in it. Anyway, good humour exuded from the gang. For perhaps an hour, none of us hated anybody or anything. Then something happened to take the edge off.

A car drove up and stopped in the middle of the street. None of us paid much attention until we heard the voice of the driver.

"By God, this is the last outrage!" roared the voice. "Here is what I sweat and slave to pay taxes for! To pay all the lazy bums in Winnipeg to sit around on the boulevards! Well, by God, I've had enough. I'm going to the mayor. I'm going to the newspapers! Who's in charge here?"

The next thing any of us knew, another voice was doing the shouting. It came from one of our gang. He had grabbed the taxpayer's tie and pulled his head through the open window of the car. Their noses were perhaps a foot apart and a dandelion knife was pointed at the taxpayer's chin.

Months of pent-up resentment against life on relief was exploding in a torrent of curses and threats. For artistry in cursing and variety of epithet, it was a *tour de force*, incapable of expurgation.

He was not, he said, a bum. He was a railroad fireman, but

73

because the country was being run by — stupid people like this — taxpayer, he could not hold even a — wiper's job in the — shops. And we were not being paid, not one — dime. We took jobs like this because we were afraid of getting cut off relief.

The taxpayer's indignation turned to panic. He tried to loosen the grip on his tie, but our champion jabbed his hand with the dandelion digger and his resistance collapsed. Our man went on:

The taxpayer was not going to report anyone to anybody. He was going to get the hell off the street, and if he so much as let out a peep to anyone, there were twenty guys here who would have his licence number and who had all the spare time required to make him live to regret it.

He released the taxpayer and gave his face a vigorous push back through the open window. As the car moved off to a chorus of loud jeers, he held his dandelion knife firmly against the body. So far as I know, the incident was never reported. None of us were as tired when the foreman came around and handed out the car-tickets that night.

It rained the next day, so we were sent home early. That was my one and only experience on the boulevard sector of the dandelion offensive. Apparently there had been trouble on other streets, for the boulevard campaign was ended and a new front opened in the city parks.

None of us minded the park work. Assiniboine Park was always a wonderful place to spend a day. After Labour Day it was almost empty of visitors and we had the place to ourselves. Later on, when the frost came, we exchanged our dandelion knives for rakes and turned our attention to the leaves. We raked enough leaves that fall to keep the park in compost for years. Raking leaves was a pleasant pastime, and whenever the foreman wasn't looking we'd start a bonfire and toast our posteriors while we enjoyed the aroma of burning leaves. Leaf-raking was not without its compensations.

One of the more curious aspects of the state of mind behind

the boondoggles was the limited scope of the imagination. Weird and wonderful schemes of organized time-wasting were dreamed up for the manual labourers, but there was nothing for anybody else. Labourers had certainly been in the majority in the beginning, but they were eventually superseded by skilled artisans, clerks, book-keepers, and white-collar workers in their infinite varieties.

On the work-gangs and at the Woodyard, we kidded around about being discriminated against. Why not some work for us to keep in practice, like adding up the numbers in telephone books, or keeping books in invisible ink? Low-grade satire it might have been, but from what transpired it was easy to suspect that somebody had been eavesdropping. One day in 1932 we were solemnly directed into a new line at the Woodyard. It ended at a table at which a battery of clerks were seated. Each of us was handed a printed promissory note in favour of the City of Winnipeg. We signed the note, solemnly promising to repay the city for the full cost of relief being given to us. The clerks duly witnessed our signatures and deposited the notes in a large drawer.

The episode was of course treated as a huge joke, which it was. Bales of notes were collected and I often wondered what would have happened if the city treasurer had taken them into the bank and offered them as security on which to borrow enough to pay the bill for printing them. There is little doubt what the answer would have been. The notes were filed and forgotten and that was the end of them. But it was far from the end of the boondoggling, which lasted as long as the Depression itself.

SASKATCHEWAN
William W. Smith

Capo - 1st Position
Chords in Key of E
Capo - 1ère position
Accords en ton de mi

Sas - kat - che-wan, the land of snow Where winds are al - ways on the blow, Where peo - ple sit with fro - zen toes, And why we stay here no one knows.

REFRAIN Sas - kat - che-wan, Sas - kat - che-wan, There's no place like Sas - kat - che-wan. We sit and gaze a - cross the plain, And won - der why it ne - ver rains, And Ga - briel blows his trum - pet sound; He says: "The rain, she's gone a - round."

Collected by Edith Fowke.

2. Our pigs are dying on their feet
     Because they have no feed to eat;
   Our horses, though of bronco race,
     Starvation stares them in the face.

   Refrain

3. The milk from cows has ceased to flow,
     We've had to ship them east, you know;
   Our hens are old and lay no eggs,
     Our turkeys eat grasshopper legs.

   Refrain

4. But still we love Saskatchewan,
     We're proud to say we're native ones,
   So count your blessings drop by drop,
     Next year we'll have a bumper crop!

   Refrain

WAS IT GOD'S PUNISHMENT?
Barry Broadfoot (ed.)

"Millions, billions, trillions. Yes, I remember grasshoppers. They would stop the trains. No traction. What a country! Dust would stop the trains and cars. The engineer couldn't see his bell and the car driver couldn't see the ornament on his water tank at the front of the hood.

But grasshoppers. Trillions. They would black out the sky and when they passed, nothing would be left. I've seen an ordinary kitchen broom leaning up against the side of a granary where we were crushing oats and when the hoppers were finished, all that was left of that broom was the handle and you couldn't tell it had been a handle because it was so chewed up except for the metal band which kept the bristles held together. Grasshoppers didn't eat machinery, but by God, I've seen them eat the leather off the seat of a John Deere tractor."

CREDIT

F. R. Scott

This delegation of unemployed Canadians
Had just been informed
That if the Government spent any more on relief
So that their children might be decently clothed and fed
The credit of the country would suffer.

FRIENDS, ROMANS, HUNGRYMEN

A. M. Klein

So one day, way back in the time of the fairytales, the boss called me into his cave and said that he was sorry but he was going to lay me off. He said it nicely, like an ogre elocuting fee-fi-fo-fum. He grabbed me, wrapped me up in a little package, and laid me down upon a dusty shelf. Then he stuck out a long tongue, licked the gluey side of a strip of paper, pasted it on me, and read it over: Unemployed.

At night, when I heard no more belches in the cave, I knew the boss had gone home for a refill of his belching stuff. He is a sick man, he always eats. I wriggled out of the package, and went to the park. I applied for membership in the zoo.

I have been there ever since.

Sometimes I am very hungry. Things in my stomach toy about with my intestines, pulling them out like elastic, and letting them go snap.

At those times, I go through the lanes of the city. I lift the haloes from off the garbage-cans, and always find a tid-bit. Manna. It tastes like whatever one wishes it to taste. I only want it to taste like food.

Once I realized that it would be a long time before I would get a real meal. So I took out my false teeth, polished them on my cuff and wrapped them in a piece of cellophane that I picked up in the street on a cigarette box. Soon I put the teeth back into my mouth. The better to smile with, my child.

I smile to the dames that pass through the park. They look good, and when they are gone, a sweet smell still floats in the air. But they never give me a tumble. I think I am too skinny. They don't like ethereal guys.

It is terrible not to have a roof over your head. All day, white molten lead is poured over me from a big cauldron which somebody on purpose hangs up in the sky.

At night I sleep on a bench in the park. A lot of other bums do the same. Before I fall asleep, I always watch the shadowy cobras, and the prowling leopards coming towards me. In the morning I wake up, and my shoes and cap are wet from the licking of the beasts.

My head is getting duller and duller. It feels like a cage in which mice are scampering about looking for cheese that isn't there. It is because I am getting so stupid that I was nearly run over by Ezekiel's chariot which came rushing at me, stinking like a field of over-ripe radishes, and screaming with the voice of a dinosaur. I was picked up from the gutter, sugared with dust like a Turkish delight.

As I turned a street corner, I met God. I asked Him for a dime for a cup of coffee. He told me He had no small change, but recommended to me a swell flophouse on the Milky Way. Then, as an afterthought He put His hand in His pocket, and took out a couple of cheap comets. Because my pockets are torn, I tied one up in my shirt, lit the other, and strolled down the boulevard, puffing like a plutocrat.

There is nothing like a bit of self-confidence. I went back to the boss who was swathed in many rolls of pork-loins. I asked him for my job. He said: Can't you see that you are lying on a shelf? Go away from here, you are a ghost. I pushed my fingers between my ribs and pulled out my heart, and said: Look, it is going. It's a fake, he answered, you just wound it up.

After that I had to take a drink. I drank at a public fountain. But I did not enjoy it. A creature, with two arms, two legs, a wooden fang, and growing blue wool all over him, kept watching me. And when I stopped to wipe my lips with my sleeve, he said — in English — Move on.

The best is to sit on a bench in the park. There are all kinds of papers lying around, and if you are not tired, you can read them, for nothing. I like to read the menus. Yesterday, I picked up a nifty, and the birds who were looking over my shoulder sang, *Fricassee! Fricassee! Pâté de foie gras!*

But you get rubbed out sitting too much. Some day I will have to sit on my sixteenth vertebra. I look around. There is a sign which says KEEP OFF THE GRASS, but the sign itself breaks the rule. So I lie down on my belly, and watch the ant-hills. I have nothing to do. I give every ant a name, names of fellows who used to work with me in the office. The fat ant is

Bill the accountant, the skinny one is the office boy, Fred, and the one with the shaking head is Old Man Harris, the Credit manager. I envy the ants. They all have jobs.

Did you ever come to think that birds and beasts are always employed? They all have jobs. They are always doing something. They are laid off only when they are dead. That's civilization for you.

And the birds that work all summer go to Miami for the winter. Even the squirrels save up their nuts for a snowy day. Perhaps the boss kept something for me, to give me when he laid me off. I went to him, and asked him for my ten kegs of sweat which he was keeping back. The boss pulled up his lips, and showed me his teeth. I heard noises going on in his throat.

That night I dreamed I was up in the sky. I picked bright blueberries out of its floor, and ate them. Then I washed it all down by drinking a bucketful that I pulled up from a well of golden soup.

But in the morning my mouth was dry. A kind lady gave me a sandwich. I took it to the park and ate it. All the bums pointed their fingers at me, singing: Shame! Shame! He's ea-ting! He's ea-ting!

The benchers of the park say that the trouble with the system is that there are not enough coins in circulation. They are going to issue some of their own. They had a fight about whose map to put on the ducats. Big Tom wants his face there, but Sam says he looks nicer. Somebody suggested an Indian's head. Naw, we don't want no foreigners.

Then somebody said that it would be better to have a symbol. No, a face. No, a symbol. Alright, a face and a symbol. So it was decided that we put a skull, anybody's skull, on the coin. Now we have to find the metal.

I have no faith in their plans. I would like to be a sweeper in the mint.

On the park bench I found a newspaper. I noticed one page on which the printer had forgotten to set any type; then in the corner I observed a number of bugs arrayed in a funny

82

combination on the blank paper. They weren't bugs: it said Man Wanted. I went to the place. The man at the door said: You have a late edition, buddy, that was a month ago.

I scrammed. On the way I met my cousin Gerald. He stopped his car, and undid the top buttons of his pants. It's tough, he said, and caught his breath. I said yes. Why don't you go into business for yourself, he said. That's a good idea, I said. I am going to get a sky-rocket and shoot up to the moon. I will take the moon off its hinges, and hide it somewhere. I will say: You want moonlight, pay. Then I will rent the moon out at so much per night. Cut rates for sweethearts. Then I will organize a company and sell moonbeam shares. Yes, I will go into business for myself. Anyway, give me your paper.

In the paper there was a headline, with a big fat exclamation mark: There is a job! When it came my turn to see the guy who was looking over the candidates, I said: Gotta job? It must have sounded foolish, after me waiting in line for so long. Gotta job? How much am I offered, he said.

I went back to the park. I threw my soul into a thimble which a nursemaid had lost under a bench. I planted the thing in the earth. I spat upon it; I said: Let it grow.

And now, now I want to die. The bums in the park had a long talk about suicide. They said to me: If you want to die so much, why don't you throw yourself from a sky-scraper?

I haven't enough weight to hurt myself, I said.

How about poison?

I *have* eaten in relief joints, I said.

Ah, they said, shooting?

That's to kill healthy men with.

Then they got sore. Go and hang yourself, they said.

I got sore, too. You dumb clucks, I said, can't you see my neck's too thin not to slip out of any knot?

Somebody said, Have you tried starving? when a guy who was eavesdropping on us, jumped on a bench and shouted: Friends, Romans, hungrymen, lend me your tears. Then he threw his arms up in the air, and pushed out his chest, on which his arms landed when they fell. Then he craned his neck this way and that, and asked a lot of questions, and didn't wait for an answer. We lent him our tears, and he wept.

Suddenly there appeared a herd of those same creatures that once mooed me away from the fountain. They were grabbing the boys by their manes, and pushing them into a wagon. One of them bit me over the head with a wooden fang, and dragged me to a station. That is the name of the lair of these creatures.

Then I was stood before a head which was lying on an open code, and the head said that somebody had overheard me talking about suicide. This was a crime, the head said, and screamed numbers at me. My life belonged to the state. I felt very proud because they were making a fuss about me killing myself.

Then the head said that I would be charged in due course with attempt at suicide and disturbing the peace. In the meantime, if I wanted to make a statement, I didn't have to, and if I didn't want to make a statement, I might. Or something like that. Then somebody gave me pen and ink.

That's how I come to write down everything that I have written down. I am very happy because they tell me that I am going to jail. I hear that they have meals there, regular.

And I hear too that they have work. They even make you work. Imagine! Nobody says how much am I offered?

I hope I stay there forever and forever, amen. This is my statement.

DAY AND NIGHT
Dorothy Livesay

I

Dawn, red and angry, whistles loud and sends
A geysered shaft of steam searching the air.
Scream after scream announces that the churn
Of life must move, the giant arm command.
Men in a stream, a human moving belt
Move into sockets, every one a bolt.
The fun begins, a humming whirring drum —
Men do a dance in time to the machines.

One step forward
Two steps back
Shove the lever,
Push it back

While Arnot whirls
A roundabout
And Geoghan shuffles
Bolts about

One step forward
Hear it crack
Smashing rhythm —
Two steps back.

Your heart-beat pounds
Against your throat
The roaring voices
Drown your shout

Across the way
A writhing whack
Sets you spinning
Two steps back —

One step forward
Two steps back.

II

Day and night rising and falling
Night and day shift gears and slip rattling
Down the runway, shot into storerooms
Where only eyes and a notebook remember
The record of evil, the sum of commitments.
We move as through sleep's revolving memories
Piling up hatred, stealing the remnants
Doors forever folding before us —
And where is the recompense, on what agenda
Will you set love down? Who knows of peace?

Day and night
Night and day
Light rips into ribbons
What we say

I called to love
Deep in dream:
Be with me in the daylight
As in gloom.

Be with me in the pounding
In the knives against my back
Set your voice resounding
Above the steel's whip crack.

High and sweet
Sweet and high
Hold, hold up the sunlight
In the sky!

Day and night
Night and day
Tear up all the silence
Find the words I could not say . . .

III

We were stoking coal in the furnaces; red hot
They gleamed, burning our skins away, his and mine.
We were working together, night and day, and knew
Each other's stroke; and without words exchanged
An understanding about kids at home,
The landlord's jaw, wage-cuts and overtime.

We were like buddies, see? Until they said
That nigger is too smart the way he smiles
And sauces back the foreman; he might say
Too much one day, to others changing shifts.
Therefore they cut him down, who flowered at night
And raised me up, day hanging over night —
So furnaces could still consume our withered skin.

Shadrack, Mechak and Abednego
Turn in the furnace, whirling slow.

    Lord, I'm burnin' in the fire
    Lord, I'm steppin' on the coal
    Lord, I'm blacker than my brother
    Blow your breath down here.

    Boss, I'm smothered in the darkness
    Boss, I'm shrivellin' in the flames
    Boss, I'm blacker than my brother
    Blow your breath down here.

Shadrack, Mechak and Abednego
Burn in the furnace, whirling slow.

    IV

Up in the roller room, men swing steel
Swing it, zoom; and cut it, crash.
Up in the dark the welder's torch
Makes sparks fly like lightning's reel.

Now I remember storm on a field:
The trees bow tense before the blow
Even the jittering sparrow's talk
Ripples into the still tree shield.

We are in storm that has no cease
No lull before, no after time
When green with rain the grasses grow
And air is sweet with fresh increase.

We bear the burden home to bed
The furnace glows within our hearts:
Our bodies hammered through the night
Are welded into bitter bread.

Bitter, yes:
But listen, friend,
We are mightier
In the end

We have ears
Alert to seize
A weakness in
The foreman's ease.

We have eyes
To look across
The bosses' profit
At our loss.

Are you waiting?
Wait with us
Every evening
There's a hush

Use it not
For love's slow count:
Add up hate
And let it mount —

One step forward
Two steps back
Will soon be over:
Hear it crack!

The wheels may whirr
A roundabout
And neighbour's shuffle
Drown your shout

The wheel must limp
Till it hangs still
And crumpled men
Pour down the hill:

Day and night
Night and day —
Till life is turned
The other way!

HUNGER

Raymond Souster

After you lay the quarter down and have a meal,
Wipe your mouth with a paper napkin and walk out of the
    lunch-room,
Your head higher, your body stronger, your heart lighter,
    because you have eaten,
Because you have done again what people do when they feel
    hungry,

How long will you walk on air, how long will you smile at the
    world, this beloved plot of earth,
Before you remember what a man with empty pockets
    remembers, fears, goes crazy remembering
As night comes, and the streets are dark and cold, and you are
    alone with the sound of your feet on the pavements,
The pain in your belly like a thousand needles jabbing,
How long will you panhandle like the blind man on the corner,
    how long will you take it before you steal, before you attack,
    before you kill?

WALKER BROTHERS COWBOY

Alice Munro

After supper my father says, "Want to go down and see if the Lake's still there?" We leave my mother sewing under the dining-room light, making clothes for me against the opening of school. She has ripped up for this purpose an old suit and an old plaid wool dress of hers, and she has to cut and match very cleverly and also make me stand and turn for endless fittings, sweaty, itching from the hot wool, ungrateful. We leave my brother in bed in the little screened porch at the end of the front verandah, and sometimes he kneels on his bed and presses his face against the screen and calls mournfully, "Bring me an ice cream cone!" but I call back, "You will be asleep," and do not even turn my head.

Then my father and I walk gradually down a long, shabby sort of street, with Silverwoods Ice Cream signs standing on the sidewalk, outside tiny, lighted stores. This is in Tuppertown, an old town on Lake Huron, an old grain port. The street is shaded, in some places, by maple trees whose roots have cracked and heaved the sidewalk and spread out like crocodiles into the bare yards. People are sitting out, men in shirt-sleeves and undershirts and women in aprons — not people we know but if anybody looks ready to nod and say, "Warm night," my father will nod too and say something the same. Children are still playing. I don't know them either because my mother keeps my brother and me in our own yard, saying he is too young to leave it and I have to mind him. I am not so sad to watch their evening games because the games themselves are ragged, dissolving. Children, of their own will, draw apart, separate into islands of two or one under the heavy trees, occupying themselves in such solitary ways as I do all day, planting pebbles in the dirt or writing in it with a stick.

Presently we leave these yards and houses behind, we pass a factory with boarded-up windows, a lumberyard whose high wooden gates are locked for the night. Then the town falls away in a defeated jumble of sheds and small junkyards, the sidewalk gives up and we are walking on a sandy path with burdocks, plantains, humble nameless weeds all around. We enter a vacant lot, a kind of park really, for it is kept clear of junk and there is one bench with a slat missing on the back, a place to sit and look at the water. Which is generally grey in the evening, under a lightly overcast sky, no sunsets, the horizon dim. A very quiet, washing noise on the stones of the beach. Further along, towards the main part of town, there is a stretch of sand, a water slide, floats bobbing around the safe swimming area, a life guard's rickety throne. Also a long dark green building, like a roofed verandah, called the Pavilion, full of farmers and their wives, in stiff good clothes, on Sundays. That is the part of the town we used to know when we lived at Dungannon and came here three or four times a summer, to the Lake. That, and the docks where we would go and look at the grain boats, ancient, rusty, wallowing, making us wonder how they got past the breakwater let alone to Fort William.

Tramps hang around the docks and occasionally on these evenings wander up the dwindling beach and climb the shifting, precarious path boys have made, hanging onto dry bushes, and say something to my father which, being frightened of tramps, I am too alarmed to catch. My father says he is a bit hard up himself. "I'll roll you a cigarette if it's any use to you," he says, and he shakes tobacco out carefully on one of the thin butterfly papers, flicks it with his tongue, seals it and hands it to the tramp who takes it and walks away. My father also rolls and lights and smokes one cigarette of his own.

He tells me how the Great Lakes came to be. All where Lake Huron is now, he says, used to be flat land, a wide flat plain. Then came the ice, creeping down from the north, pushing deep into the low places. Like *that* — and he shows me his hand with his spread fingers pressing the rock-hard ground where we are sitting. His fingers make hardly any impression at all and he says, "Well, the old ice cap had a lot more power behind it than this hand has." And then the ice went back, shrank back towards the North Pole where it came from, and left its fingers of ice in the deep places it had gouged, and ice turned to lakes and there they were today. They were *new*, as time went. I try to see that plain before me, dinosaurs walking on it, but I am not able even to imagine the shore of the Lake when the Indians were there, before Tuppertown. The tiny share we have of time appalls me, though my father seems to regard it with tranquillity. Even my father, who sometimes seems to me to have been at home in the world as long as it has lasted, has really lived on this earth only a little longer than I have, in terms of all the time there has been to live in. He has not known a time, any more than I, when automobiles and electric lights did not at least exist. He was not alive when this century started. I will be barely alive — old, old — when it ends. I do not like to think of it. I wish the Lake to be always just a lake, with the safe-swimming floats marking it, and the breakwater and the lights of Tuppertown.

My father has a job, selling for Walker Brothers. This is a firm that sells almost entirely in the country, the back country. Sunshine, Boylesbridge, Turnaround — that is all his territory. Not Dungannon where we used to live, Dungannon is too near town and my mother is grateful for that. He sells cough medicine, iron tonic, corn plasters, laxatives, pills for female disorders, mouth wash, shampoo, liniment, salves, lemon and orange and raspberry concentrate for making refreshing drinks, vanilla, food colouring, black and green tea, ginger, cloves and other spices, rat poison. He has a song about it, with these two lines:

> And have all liniments and oils,
> For everything from corns to boils. . . .

Not a very funny song, in my mother's opinion. A pedlar's song, and that is what he is, a pedlar knocking at backwoods kitchens. Up until last winter we had our own business, a fox farm. My father raised silver foxes and sold their pelts to the

94

people who make them into capes and coats and muffs. Prices fell, my father hung on hoping they would *get better next year*, and they fell again, and he hung on one more year and one more and finally it was not possible to hang on any more, we owed everything to the feed company. I have heard my mother explain this, several times, to Mrs. Oliphant who is the only neighbour she talks to. (Mrs. Oliphant also has come down in the world, being a schoolteacher who married the janitor.) We poured all we had into it, my mother says, and we came out with nothing. Many people could say the same thing, these days, but my mother has no time for the national calamity, only ours. Fate has flung us onto a street of poor people (it does not matter that we were poor before, that was a different sort of poverty), and the only way to take this, as she sees it, is with dignity, with bitterness, with no reconciliation. No bathroom with a claw-footed tub and a flush toilet is going to comfort her, nor water on tap and sidewalks past the house and milk in bottles, not even the two movie theatres and the Venus Restaurant and Woolworth's so marvellous it has live birds singing in its fan-cooled corners and fish as tiny as fingernails, as bright as moons, swimming in its green tanks. My mother does not care.

In the afternoons she often walks to Simon's Grocery and takes me with her to help carry things. She wears a good dress, navy blue with little flowers, sheer, worn over a navy-blue slip. Also a summer hat of white straw, pushed down on the side of the head, and white shoes I have just whitened on a newspaper on the back steps. I have my hair freshly done in long damp curls which the dry air will fortunately soon loosen, a stiff large hair-ribbon on top of my head. This is entirely different from going out after supper with my father. We have not walked past two houses before I feel we have become objects of universal ridicule. Even the dirty words chalked on the sidewalk are laughing at us. My mother does not seem to notice. She walks serenely like a lady shopping, like a *lady* shopping, past the housewives in loose beltless dresses torn under the arms. With me her creation, wretched curls and flaunting hair bow, scrubbed knees and white socks — all I do not want to be. I loathe even my name when she says it in public, in a voice so high, proud and ringing, deliberately different from the voice of any other mother on the street.

My mother will sometimes carry home, for a treat, a brick of ice cream — pale Neapolitan; and because we have no refrigerator in our house we wake my brother and eat it at once in the dining room, always darkened by the wall of the house next door. I spoon it up tenderly, leaving the chocolate till last, hoping to have some still to eat when my brother's dish is empty. My mother tries then to imitate the conversations we used to have at Dungannon, going back to our earliest, most leisurely days before my brother was born, when she would give me a little tea and a lot of milk in a cup like hers and we would sit out on the step facing the pump, the lilac tree, the fox pens beyond. She is not able to keep from mentioning those days. "Do you remember when we put you in your sled and Major pulled you?" (Major our dog, that we had to leave with neighbours when we moved.) "Do you remember your sandbox outside the kitchen window?" I pretend to remember far less than I do, wary of being trapped into sympathy or any unwanted emotion.

My mother has headaches. She often has to lie down. She lies on my brother's narrow bed in the little screened porch, shaded by heavy branches. "I look up at that tree and I think I am at home," she says.

"What you need," my father tells her, "is some fresh air and a drive in the country." He means for her to go with him, on his Walker Brothers route.

That is not my mother's idea of a drive in the country.

"Can I come?"

"Your mother might want you for trying on clothes."

"I'm beyond sewing this afternoon," my mother says.

"I'll take her then. Take both of them, give you a rest."

What is there about us that people need to be given a rest from? Never mind. I am glad enough to find my brother and make him go to the toilet and get us both into the car, our knees unscrubbed, my hair unringleted. My father brings from the house his two heavy brown suitcases, full of bottles, and sets them on the back seat. He wears a white shirt, brilliant in the sunlight, a tie, light trousers belonging to his summer suit (his other suit is black, for funerals, and belonged to my uncle before he died) and a creamy straw hat. His salesman's outfit, with pencils clipped in the shirt pocket. He goes back once again, probably to say goodbye to my mother, to ask her if she is sure she doesn't want to come, and hear her say, "No. No thanks, I'm better just to lie here with my eyes closed." Then we are backing out of the driveway with the rising hope of adventure, just the little hope that takes you over the bump into the street, the hot air starting to move, turning into a breeze, the houses growing less and less familiar as we follow the short cut my father knows, the quick way out of town. Yet what is there waiting for us all afternoon but hot hours in stricken farmyards, perhaps a stop at a country store and three ice cream cones or bottles of pop, and my father singing? The one he made up about himself has a title — "The Walker Brothers Cowboy" — and it starts out like this:

Old Ned Fields, he now is dead,
So I am ridin' the route instead. . . .

Who is Ned Fields? The man he has replaced, surely, and if so he really is dead; yet my father's voice is mournful-jolly, making his death some kind of nonsense, a comic calamity. "Wisht I was back on the Rio Grande, plungin' through the dusky sand." My father sings most of the time while driving the car. Even now, heading out of town, crossing the bridge and taking the sharp turn onto the highway, he is humming something, mumbling a bit of a song to himself, just tuning up, really, getting ready to improvise, for out along the highway we pass the Baptist Camp, the Vacation Bible Camp, and he lets loose:

> Where are the Baptists, where are the Baptists,
> where are all the Baptists today?
> They're down in the water, in Lake Huron water,
> with their sins all a-gittin' washed away.

My brother takes this for straight truth and gets up on his knees trying to see down to the Lake. "I don't see any Baptists," he says accusingly. "Neither do I, son," says my father. "I told you, they're down in the Lake."

No roads paved when we left the highway. We have to roll up the windows because of dust. The land is flat, scorched, empty. Bush lots at the back of the farms hold shade, black pine-shade like pools nobody can ever get to. We bump up a long lane and at the end of it what could look more unwelcoming, more deserted than the tall unpainted farmhouse with grass growing uncut right up to the front door, green blinds down and a door upstairs opening on nothing but air? Many houses have this door, and I have never yet been able to find out why. I ask my father and he says they are for walking in your sleep. *What?* Well if you happen to be walking in your sleep and you want to step outside. I am offended, seeing too late that he is joking, as usual, but my brother says sturdily, "If they did that they would break their necks."

The nineteen-thirties. How much this kind of farmhouse, this kind of afternoon, seem to me to belong to that one decade in time, just as my father's hat does, his bright flared tie, our car with its wide running board (an Essex, and long past its prime). Cars somewhat like it, many older, none dustier, sit in the farmyards. Some are past running and have their doors pulled off, their seats removed for use on porches. No living things to be seen, chickens or cattle. Except dogs. There are dogs, lying in any kind of shade they can find, dreaming, their lean sides rising and sinking rapidly. They get up when my father opens the car door, he has to speak to them. "Nice boy, there's a boy, nice old boy." They quiet down, go back to their shade. He should know how to quiet animals, he has held desperate foxes with tongs around their necks. One gentling voice for the dogs and another, rousing, cheerful, for calling at doors. "Hello there, Missus, it's the Walker Brothers man and what are you out of today?" A door opens, he disappears. Forbidden to follow, forbidden even to leave the car, we can just wait and wonder what he says. Sometimes trying to make my mother laugh he pretends to be himself in a farm kitchen, spreading out his sample case. "Now then, Missus, are you troubled with parasitic life? Your children's scalps, I mean. All those crawly little things we're too polite to mention that show up on the heads of the best of families? Soap alone is useless, kerosene is not too nice a perfume, but I have here — " Or else, "Believe me, sitting and driving all day the way I do I *know* the value of these fine pills. Natural relief. A problem common to old folks, too, once their days of activity are over — How about you, Grandma?" He would wave the imaginary box of pills under my mother's nose and she would laugh finally, unwillingly. "He doesn't say that really, does he?" I said, and she said no of course not, he was too much of a gentleman.

One yard after another, then, the old cars, the pumps, dogs, views of grey barns and falling-down sheds and unturning windmills. The men, if they are working in the fields, are not in any fields that we can see. The children are far away, following dry creek beds or looking for blackberries, or else they are hidden in the house, spying at us through cracks in the blinds. The car seat has grown slick with our sweat. I dare my brother to sound the horn, wanting to do it myself but not wanting to get the blame. He knows better. We play *I Spy*, but it is hard to find many colours. Grey for the barns and sheds and toilets and houses, brown for the yard and fields, black or brown for the dogs. The rusting cars show rainbow patches, in which I strain to pick out purple or green; likewise I peer at doors for shreds of old peeling paint, maroon or yellow. We can't play with letters, which would be better, because my brother is too young to spell. The game disintegrates anyway. He claims my colours are not fair, and wants extra turns.

In one house no door opens, though the car is in the yard. My father knocks and whistles, calls, "Hullo there! Walker Brothers man!" but there is not a stir of reply anywhere. This house has no porch, just a bare, slanting slab of cement on which my father stands. He turns around, searching the barnyard, the barn whose mow must be empty because you can see the sky through it, and finally he bends to pick up his suitcases. Just then a window is opened upstairs, a white pot appears on the sill, is tilted over and its contents splash down the outside wall. The window is not directly above my father's head, so only a stray splash would catch him. He picks up his suitcases with no particular hurry and walks, no longer whistling, to the car. "Do you know what that was?" I say to my brother. *"Pee."* He laughs and laughs.

My father rolls and lights a cigarette before he starts the car. The window has been slammed down, the blind drawn, we never did see a hand or face. "Pee, pee," sings my brother ecstatically. "Somebody dumped down pee!" "Just don't tell your mother that," my father says. "She isn't liable to see the joke." "Is it in your song?" my brother wants to know. My father says no but he will see what he can do to work it in.

I notice in a little while that we are not turning in any more lanes, though it does not seem to me that we are headed home. "Is this the way to Sunshine?" I ask my father, and he answers, "No ma'am it's not." "Are we still in your territory?" He shakes his head. "We're going *fast*," my brother says approvingly, and in fact we are bouncing along through dry puddle-holes so that all the bottles in the suitcases clink together and gurgle promisingly.

Another lane, a house, also unpainted, dried to silver in the sun.

"I thought we were out of your territory."

"We are."

"Then what are we going in here for?"

"You'll see."

In front of the house a short, sturdy woman is picking up washing, which had been spread on the grass to bleach and dry. When the car stops she stares at it hard for a moment, bends to pick up a couple more towels to add to the bundle under her arm, comes across to us and says in a flat voice, neither welcoming nor unfriendly, "Have you lost your way?"

My father takes his time getting out of the car. "I don't think so," he says. "I'm the Walker Brothers man."

"George Golley is our Walker Brothers man," the woman says, "and he was out here no more than a week ago. Oh, my Lord God," she says harshly, "it's you."

"It was, the last time I looked in the mirror," my father says. The woman gathers all the towels in front of her and holds on to them tightly, pushing them against her stomach as if it hurt. "Of all the people I never thought to see. And telling me you were the Walker Brothers man."

"I'm sorry if you were looking forward to George Golley," my father says humbly.

"And look at me, I was prepared to clean the hen-house. You'll think that's just an excuse but it's true. I don't go round looking like this every day." She is wearing a farmer's straw hat, through which pricks of sunlight penetrate and float on her face, a loose, dirty print smock and running shoes. "Who are those in the car, Ben? They're not yours?"

"Well I hope and believe they are," my father says, and tells our names and ages. "Come on, you can get out. This is Nora, Miss Cronin. Nora, you better tell me, is it still Miss, or have you got a husband hiding in the woodshed?"

"If I had a husband that's not where I'd keep him, Ben," she says, and they both laugh, her laugh abrupt and somewhat angry. "You'll think I got no manners, as well as being dressed like a tramp," she says. "Come on in out of the sun. It's cool in the house."

We go across the yard ("Excuse me taking you in this way but I don't think the front door has been opened since Papa's funeral, I'm afraid the hinges might drop off"), up the porch steps, into the kitchen, which really is cool, high-ceilinged, the blinds of course down, a simple, clean, threadbare room with waxed worn linoleum, potted geraniums, drinking-pail and dipper, a round table with scrubbed oilcloth. In spite of the cleanness, the wiped and swept surfaces, there is a faint sour smell — maybe of the dishrag or the tin dipper or the oilcloth, or the old lady, because there is one, sitting in an easy chair under the clock shelf. She turns her head slightly in our direction and says, "Nora? Is that company?"

"Blind," says Nora in a quick explaining voice to my father. Then, "You won't guess who it is, Momma. Hear his voice."

My father goes to the front of her chair and bends and says hopefully, "Afternoon, Mrs. Cronin."

"Ben Jordan," says the old lady with no surprise. "You haven't been to see us in the longest time. Have you been out of the country?"

My father and Nora look at each other.

"He's married, Momma," says Nora cheerfully and aggressively. "Married and got two children and here they are." She pulls us forward, makes each of us touch the old lady's dry, cool hand while she says our names in turn. Blind! This is the first blind person I have ever seen close up. Her eyes are closed, the eyelids sunk away down, showing no shape of the eyeball, just hollows. From one hollow comes a drop of silver liquid, a medicine, or a miraculous tear.

"Let me get into a decent dress," Nora says. "Talk to Momma. It's a treat for her. We hardly ever see company, do we Momma?"

"Not many makes it out this road," says the old lady placidly. "And the ones that used to be around here, our old neighbours, some of them have pulled out."

"True everywhere," my father says.

"Where's your wife then?"

"Home. She's not too fond of the hot weather, makes her feel poorly."

"Well." This is a habit of country people, old people, to say "well", meaning, "is that so?" with a little extra politeness and concern.

Nora's dress, when she appears again — stepping heavily on Cuban heels down the stairs in the hall — is flowered more lavishly than anything my mother owns, green and yellow on brown, some sort of floating sheer crepe, leaving her arms bare.

Her arms are heavy, and every bit of her skin you can see is covered with little dark freckles like measles. Her hair is short, black, coarse and curly, her teeth very white and strong. "It's the first time I knew there was such a thing as green poppies," my father says, looking at her dress.

"You would be surprised all the things you never knew," says Nora, sending a smell of cologne far and wide when she moves and displaying a change of voice to go with the dress, something more sociable and youthful. "They're not poppies anyway, they're just flowers. You go and pump me some good cold water and I'll make these children a drink." She gets down from the cupboard a bottle of Walker Brothers orange syrup.

"You telling me you were the Walker Brothers man!"

"It's the truth, Nora. You go and look at my sample cases in the car if you don't believe me. I got the territory directly south of here."

"Walker Brothers? Is that a fact? You selling for Walker Brothers?"

"Yes ma'am."

"We always heard you were raising foxes over Dungannon way."

"That's what I was doing, but I kind of run out of luck in that business."

"So where're you living? How long've you been out selling?"

"We moved into Tuppertown. I been at it, oh, two, three months. It keeps the wolf from the door. Keeps him as far away as the back fence."

Nora laughs. "Well I guess you count yourself lucky to have the work. Isabel's husband in Brantford, he was out of work the longest time. I thought if he didn't find something soon I was going to have them all land in here to feed, and I tell you I was hardly looking forward to it. It's all I can manage with me and Momma."

"Isabel married," my father says. "Muriel married too?"

"No, she's teaching school out west. She hasn't been home

for five years. I guess she finds something better to do with her holidays. I would if I was her." She gets some snapshots out of the table drawer and starts showing him. "That's Isabel's oldest boy, starting school. That's the baby sitting in her carriage. Isabel and her husband. Muriel. That's her room-mate with her. That's a fellow she used to go around with, and his car. He was working in a bank out there. That's her school, it has eight rooms. She teaches Grade Five." My father shakes his head. "I can't think of her any way but when she was going to school, so shy I used to pick her up on the road — I'd be on my way to see you — and she would not say one word, not even to agree it was a nice day."

"She's got over that."

"Who are you talking about?" says the old lady.

"Muriel. I said she's got over being shy."

"She was here last summer."

"No Momma that was Isabel. Isabel and her family were here last summer. Muriel's out west."

"I meant Isabel."

Shortly after this the old lady falls asleep, her head on the side, her mouth open. "Excuse her manners," Nora says. "It's old age." She fixes an afghan over her mother and says we can all go into the front room where our talking won't disturb her.

"You two," my father says. "Do you want to go outside and amuse yourselves?"

Amuse ourselves how? Anyway I want to stay. The front room is more interesting than the kitchen, though barer. There is a gramophone and a pump organ and a picture on the wall of Mary, Jesus' mother — I know that much — in shades of bright blue and pink with a spiked band of light around her head. I know that such pictures are found only in the homes of Roman Catholics and so Nora must be one. We have never known any Roman Catholics at all well, never well enough to visit in their houses. I think of what my grandmother and my Aunt Tena, over in Dungannon, used to always say to indicate that somebody was a Catholic. *So-and-so digs with the wrong foot*, they would say. *She digs with the wrong foot.* That was what they would say about Nora.

Nora takes a bottle, half full, out of the top of the organ and pours some of what is in it into the two glasses that she and my father have emptied of the orange drink.

"Keep it in case of sickness?" my father says.

"Not on your life," says Nora. "I'm never sick. I just keep it because I keep it. One bottle does me a fair time, though, because I don't care for drinking alone. Here's luck!" She and my father drink and I know what it is. Whisky. One of the things my mother has told me in our talks together is that my father never drinks whisky. But I see he does. He drinks whisky and he talks of people whose names I have never heard before. But after a while he turns to a familiar incident. He tells about the chamberpot that was emptied out the window. "Picture me there," he says, "hollering my heartiest. *Oh, lady, it's your Walker Brothers man, anybody home?*" He does himself hollering, grinning absurdly, waiting, looking up in pleased expectation and then — oh, ducking, covering his head with his arms, looking as if he begged for mercy (when he never did anything like that, I was watching), and Nora laughs, almost as hard as my brother did at the time.

"That isn't true! That's not a word true!"

"Oh, indeed it is ma'am. We have our heroes in the ranks of Walker Brothers. I'm glad you think it's funny," he says sombrely.

I ask him shyly, "Sing the song."

"What song? Have you turned into a singer on top of everything else?"

Embarrassed, my father says, "Oh, just this song I made up while I was driving around, it gives me something to do, making up rhymes."

But after some urging he does sing it, looking at Nora with a droll, apologetic expression, and she laughs so much that in places he has to stop and wait for her to get over laughing so he can go on, because she makes him laugh too. Then he does various parts of his salesman's spiel. Nora when she laughs squeezes her large bosom under her folded arms. "You're crazy," she says. "That's all you are." She sees my brother peering into the gramophone and she jumps up and goes over to him. "Here's us sitting enjoying ourselves and not giving you a thought, isn't it terrible?" she says. "You want me to put a record on, don't you? You want to hear a nice record? Can you dance? I bet your sister can, can't she?"

I say no. "A big girl like you and so good-looking and can't dance!" says Nora. "It's high time you learned. I bet you'd make a lovely dancer. Here, I'm going to put on a piece I used to dance to and even your daddy did, in his dancing days. You didn't know your daddy was a dancer, did you? Well, he is a talented man, your daddy!"

She puts down the lid and takes hold of me unexpectedly around the waist, picks up my other hand and starts making me go backwards. "This is the way, now, this is how they dance. Follow me. This foot, see. One and one-two. One and one-two. That's fine, that's lovely, don't look at your feet! Follow me, that's right, see how easy? You're going to be a lovely dancer! One and one-two. One and one-two. Ben, see your daughter dancing!" *Whispering while you cuddle near me Whispering where no one can hear me. . . .*

Round and round the linoleum, me proud, intent, Nora laughing and moving with great buoyancy, wrapping me in her strange gaiety, her smell of whisky, cologne, and sweat. Under the arms her dress is damp, and little drops form along her upper lip, hang in the soft black hairs at the corners of her mouth. She whirls me around in front of my father — causing me to stumble, for I am by no means so swift a pupil as she pretends — and lets me go, breathless.

"Dance with me, Ben."

"I'm the world's worst dancer, Nora, and you know it."

"I certainly never thought so."

"You would now."

She stands in front of him, arms hanging loose and hopeful, her breasts, which a moment ago embarrassed me with their warmth and bulk, rising and falling under her loose flowered dress, her face shining with the exercise, and delight.

"Ben."

My father drops his head and says quietly, "Not me, Nora."

So she can only go and take the record off. "I can drink alone but I can't dance alone," she says. "Unless I am a whole lot crazier than I think I am."

"Nora," says my father smiling. "You're not crazy."

"Stay for supper."

"Oh, no. We couldn't put you to the trouble."

"It's no trouble. I'd be glad of it."

"And their mother would worry. She'd think I'd turned us over in a ditch."

"Oh, well. Yes."

"We've taken a lot of your time now."

"Time," says Nora bitterly. "Will you come by ever again?"

"I will if I can," says my father.

"Bring the children. Bring your wife."

"Yes I will," says my father. "I will if I can."

When she follows us to the car he says, "You come to see us too, Nora. We're right on Grove Street, left-hand side going in, that's north, and two doors this side — east — of Baker Street."

Nora does not repeat these directions. She stands close to the car in her soft, brilliant dress. She touches the fender, making an unintelligible mark in the dust there.

On the way home my father does not buy any ice cream or pop, but he does go into a country store and get a package of licorice, which he shares with us. *She digs with the wrong foot*, I think, and the words seem sad to me as never before, dark, perverse. My father does not say anything to me about not mentioning things at home, but I know, just from the thoughtfulness, the pause when he passes the licorice, that there are things not to be mentioned. The whisky, maybe the dancing. No worry about my brother, he does not notice enough. At most he might remember the blind lady, the picture of Mary.

"Sing," my brother commands my father, but my father says gravely, "I don't know, I seem to be fresh out of songs. You watch the road and let me know if you see any rabbits."

So my father drives and my brother watches the road for rabbits and I feel my father's life flowing back from our car in the last of the afternoon, darkening and turning strange, like a landscape that has an enchantment on it, making it kindly, ordinary and familiar while you are looking at it, but changing it, once your back is turned, into something you will never know, with all kinds of weathers, and distances you cannot imagine.

When we get closer to Tuppertown the sky becomes gently overcast, as always, nearly always, on summer evenings by the Lake.

NEWS OF THE PHOENIX

A. J. M. Smith

They say the Phoenix is dying, some say dead.
Dead without issue is what one message said,
But that has been suppressed, officially denied.

I think, myself, the man who sent it lied.
In any case, I'm told, he has been shot,
As a precautionary measure, whether he did or not.

(1936)

QUESTIONS ON THE THEME:
The Depression in Canadian Literature

1.(a) Mrs. Samchuk and Mrs. Franklin, in the first two selections in the anthology, are both victims of the Depression. Compare and contrast these women, noting the characteristics of each that are, or are not, helpful in coping with her problems.

(b) With reference to these and other selections in the anthology, compile a list of the characteristics and emotions that seem to have predominated during the Depression. Which of these were forces for hope? which for despair? Can you make any generalizations about the behaviour of people during long periods of adversity?

2. Research the history of R. B. Bennett's term as Prime Minister of Canada. Which view of Bennett does history tend to support— Mrs. Franklin's or that of the speaker in "Pompous, Smug, and Rich"? How would you rate Bennett's handling of the problems of the Depression?

3. As a novelist, Morley Callaghan has used the Depression as background for his story about a marriage. Does the fictional treatment make the effects of the Depression less real? more real? Why?

Explain why you do or do not think Marthe and George will survive their period of adversity.

4. It is an accepted phenomenon of the Depression that people still alive today who lived through it remember it with great clarity and emotion. What do you find in "Outcasts" and "I Am a Transient" that helps you to account for this phenomenon?

Try to interview a person who lived through the Depression and compare his or her memories and experiences with those recorded here.

5. In "To a Generation Unemployed" the poet says, "So lie and dream your life-in-death". What kind of person is he addressing? In what ways does he suggest the Depression may end?

6. With her sharply critical poems about social conditions, Dorothy Livesay was one of the Thirties' best-known voices. In "Day and Night" there are political implications as well. Identify

the social and political criticisms Livesay is making, and with reference to other selections in this book tell whether you think the criticisms are justified.

7. What purpose did the creators of boondoggling think it would serve? Why were they mistaken?

8. F. R. Scott and A. M. Klein use satire as a device by which to express their views of society. To what extent do you find the satire in "Efficiency: 1935" and "Friends, Romans, Hungrymen" effective?

9. The Depression had a profound spiritual as well as physical effect on many people. Explain how this is exemplified in the character of Chris in "The Horses of the Night".
Refer to several other selections in this anthology in which spiritual effects are to be found and briefly summarize the nature of these effects. (Possible choices: "Holiday", "It's Good To Be Here", "Two Thieves", "Prairie", "Hunger", "Walker Brothers Cowboy".)

10. In what way might "News of the Phoenix" be interpreted as a comment on society in the Thirties? In your opinion, is the poem a fitting conclusion for an anthology on the Depression? Why or why not?

BIBLIOGRAPHY

BIOGRAPHICAL INFORMATION

Carl F. Klinck, *A Literary History of Canada: Canadian Literature in English*, University of Toronto Press

Norah Story, *The Oxford Companion to Canadian History and Literature*, Oxford University Press

William Stewart Wallace, *The Macmillan Dictionary of Canadian Biography*, Macmillan of Canada

NON-FICTION

Barry Broadfoot, *Ten Lost Years*, Doubleday

J. M. S. Careless, *The Canadians, 1867-1967* (Ch. 8), Macmillan of Canada

Ramsay Cook (ed.), *The Politics of Discontent*, University of Toronto Press

John Kenneth Galbraith, *The Great Crash, Nineteen Twenty-Nine*, Houghton-Mifflin

J. L. Granatstein and Paul Stevens (eds.), *Forum: Canadian Life and Letters, 1920-70* (selections from *Canadian Forum*), University of Toronto Press

James H. Gray, *The Winter Years*, Macmillan of Canada

Linda Grayson and Michael Bliss (eds.), *The Wretched of Canada: Letters to R. B. Bennett*, University of Toronto Press

C. Humphries, *The Great Depression* (Jackdaw), Clarke, Irwin

B. Singer, *The Great Depression*, Collier-Macmillan

J. B. Vaughan, *The Wandering Years*, Hancock House

FICTION

Earle Birney, *Down the Long Table*, New Canadian Library (NCL)

Morley Callaghan, *Morley Callaghan's Stories*, Macmillan of Canada

Morley Callaghan, *More Joy in Heaven; Such Is My Beloved; They Shall Inherit the Earth*; NCL

Hugh Garner, *Cabbagetown*, Pocket Books

Henry Kreisel, *The Rich Man*, NCL

Margaret Laurence, *A Bird in the House*, NCL

Edward McCourt, *Music at the Close*, NCL

Hugh MacLennan, *The Watch That Ends the Night*, Macmillan of
  Canada
John Marlyn, *Under the Ribs of Death*, NCL
W. O. Mitchell, *Who Has Seen the Wind*, Macmillan of Canada
Mary Peate, *Girl in a Red River Coat*, Clarke, Irwin
Sinclair Ross, *As for Me and My House*, NCL
Gabrielle Roy, *The Tin Flute*, NCL

PLAY

Gwen Pharis Ringwood, *Still Stands the House*, in Terry Angus
  (ed.), *The Prairie Experience* (*Themes in Canadian Literature*
  series), Macmillan of Canada

POEM

Anne Marriott, "The Wind Our Enemy", in Terry Angus (ed.),
  The Prairie Experience (*Themes in Canadian Literature* series),
  Macmillan of Canada

FILMS

Drylanders, black & white, 69 min., National Film Board (NFB)
The Great Depression, See Hear Now (film strip and cassette), Library
  of Canadian History
Sunshine and Eclipse, black & white, 29 min., NFB
Twilight of an Era, black & white, 29 min., NFB

67 77 87 97 08 18 28 38 48 THB 9 8 7 6 5 4 3 2 1